indian grill

Also by Smita Chandra

From Bengal to Punjab: The Cuisines of India

indian grill

The Art of Tandoori Cooking at Home

SMITA CHANDRA

THE ECCO PRESS

Copyright ©1999 by Smita Chandra

All rights reserved. The Ecco Press, 100 West Broad Street,
Hopewell, New Jersey 08525

Published simultaneously in Canada by Publishers Group West, Inc.,
Toronto, Ontario

Printed in the United States of America

Library of Congress Cataloging-in-Publication Data

Chandra, Smita.
  Indian grill: the art of tandoori cooking at home / Smita
Chandra.—1st ed.
      p. cm.
  Includes index.
  ISBN 0-88001-687-6
  1. Cookery, Indic.   2. Barbecue cookery.   I. Title.
TX724.5.I4C374   1999
641.5954—dc21   99-10935
                                                    CIP

9 8 7 6 5 4 3 2 1

FIRST EDITION 1999

INTERIOR DESIGN BY PETER BERTOLAMI

For Sanjeev, Rohan, and Varun,

who so enthusiastically support everything I do.

Contents

Acknowledgments ix

Introduction xi

Getting Prepared xvii

Appetizers and Drinks 3

Soups and Salads 17

Raitas and Chutneys 35

Chicken 53

Lamb 83

Seafood 101

Vegetables 119

Rice 151

Sauces 165

acknowledgments

there is no way I could have written this book without the unfailing support and help of my husband, Sanjeev, who tasted every recipe I tried out for this book and offered many suggestions on how to write them. My two sons, Rohan, 8, and Varun, 4, deserve special thanks for their moral support and for entertaining each other in order to give me time to work on this book. Rohan let me use his computer whenever I needed it and always had words of encouragement. Varun praised everything I cooked and offered lots of hugs.

I would like to thank my parents and my mother-in-law for their support and advice. Special thanks are extended to my mother, who has influenced my cooking in more ways than she knows and who has always been my best friend. My sisters-in-law, Mamta, Margit, Arti, and Rachna have shared their recipes with me over the years and have always encouraged me in my endeavors. My brothers Ashok, Aloak, and Ajay have always believed in me.

Thank you Nina, Peter, Cory, and Sophie for your appreciation of my cooking and for sharing your ideas and love of good food with me. Last but definitely not least, heartfelt thanks to Joanne Bain and Karen Cormier for their uplifting friendship, sympathetic ear, unflagging support, and free babysitting. Alex Cormier, 10, who has been saving up to buy this book, has given me added impetus to finish it!

introduction

i grew up in a strictly vegetarian household. A devout Hindu, my mother never allowed meat of any kind to be brought into the house, much less cooked in her kitchen. I was 17 and away at college in Delhi when I had my first taste of meat. My older brother Ashok, who had just gotten his first job and had lots of money (in my eyes, at least!) took me to a tandoori restaurant to celebrate and, as he put it, to widen my horizons. Amazed at my own daring, I ordered tandoori chicken, kabobs, and naan. The food smelled tantalizing when it arrived, but I was still hesitant to put that first forkful in my mouth. Egged on by my brother, I tried a small bite and it was love at first taste. I was completely enamored with tandoori cuisine and from then on ate it at every opportunity. Living in Delhi gave me lots of occasions to do so, since it is home to some of the best tandoori restaurants in the country. Exploring the narrow streets of Old Delhi you will find plenty of little restaurants—which in many cases are no more than tiny stalls—that serve the most incredible kabobs (cubes of meat marinated and cooked with vegetables, often on a skewer) and *rotis* (a kind of unleavened wheat bread).

Over the years, whenever I traveled to other parts of India, I always made a point of exploring local restaurants and sampling the regional cuisine. Part of the excitement was that restaurant food in India is very different from what most people eat at home. Generally speaking, there is no tradition of eating out in restaurants because Indians are very suspicious of any food not cooked at home. Tandoori restaurants are the exception, and you will find them in all parts of India.

Tandoori cooking acquires its name from the *tandoor*, a large clay oven that resembles a wide-bottomed pot with a narrow mouth sunk into the ground. The bottom of the tandoor is layered with glowing charcoal. Food to be cooked is marinated, threaded onto skewers, and lowered into the oven. The food is seared quickly by the extremely high temperatures of the tandoor and comes out moist and tender, infused with the characteristic aroma of the smoke produced by its juices falling on the coal. Building a tandoor in the kitchens of most homes is an impossible task, so authentic tandoori food is rarely cooked at home and can only be found in specialty restaurants.

This cooking technique is ancient: remains of tandoors over five thousand years old have been excavated in the Indus River valley. However, modern-day tandoori food represents a unique blend of two great cuisines: Indian and Middle Eastern. Indian culture has been shaped by successive waves of Arabs, Turks, Afghans, and Moghuls who invaded the country over the last thousand years. Babar, the founder of the last and greatest of these empires, the Moghuls, came to India in 1526 from Farghana—a small kingdom in what is now Uzbekistan. Having conquered the country, he added insult to injury by complaining bitterly about the people, the weather and, above all, the food. Writing in his memoirs, he said "... they have no good fruits, no ice or cold water, no good food or bread in their bazaars. . . ." The Moghuls promptly set out to rectify this sorry situation and developed the cuisine known as *Moghlai*, of which tandoori food is a prominent part. Indian spices and seasonings were combined with Moghul grilling techniques and a new style of cooking was created.

It seems somehow fitting that my first attempts at tandoori cooking were also the result of globe-trotting, in my case from East to West. I got married and moved to Ithaca, a small town in upstate New York, which did not even have an Indian grocery store. Homesick and longing for familiar food, I began to understand what Babar must have felt like. It rapidly became clear that if my husband and I were going to eat our favorite foods, we would have to cook them ourselves. Armed with a little charcoal grill and a couple of good Indian cookbooks, I set out to replicate the tandoori dishes that I had eaten in restaurants for years. After much trial and error, I perfected dishes like Tandoori Chicken and Seekh Kabobs on my backyard barbecue grill. It came as a revelation to me that the preparation of these dishes did not necessarily require the use of a traditional tandoor. If I covered the barbecue during most of the cooking period, uncovering it only at the end to char the food a little, I found that I could create the hot temperatures and smoky interior of a traditional tandoor.

Getting more adventurous, I decided to see what other Indian dishes I could adapt to the barbecue. I wrote numerous letters home begging for traditional and favorite recipes, which my family would obligingly mail to me in fat envelopes. I discovered that most Indian dishes could easily be cooked on the grill. The smoky char and aroma adds a distinctive, authentic touch. Except for the affluent, who use gas stoves, most people in India still use wood and charcoal as fuel. Enter a village when the evening meal is being cooked and you will notice the unmistakable smell of wood smoke in the air, which also permeates the food.

Cooking on my charcoal grill brought back vivid memories of my grandmother's kitchen. Her cooking was all done on the floor with her *angithi*, a little earthenware stove fueled by charcoal, with all her implements and supplies close beside her. She would sit on her *patla*, a small wooden footstool, and make rotis while the rest of the family sat in a semicircle around her. She would roast the rotis directly on the hot coals of the angithi and put them on our plates by turn. When the day's cooking was done, she would bury potatoes and eggplant in the dying embers to roast for the next day's meal. The delicious smoky aromas of her kitchen are always with me whenever I fire up my barbecue and cook a meal for my family.

When I described my culinary experiments to my mother she was pleased to see her vegetable recipes being put to good use, although she was still wary of actually eating anything cooked on the barbecue. However, when vegetarian friends came over for a barbecue, I now had something else for them besides corn on the cob and veggie burgers. Also, if I grew more tomatoes than I knew what to do with, I would make grilled chutneys and bottle or freeze them. It was always a treat to savor that barbecued flavor in the middle of winter. I also found it easy enough to throw on extra meat or vegetables at the end of a barbecue to use later in sauces, soups, or salads.

It is only when bad weather strikes that you notice the die-hard barbe-cuer. My husband and I are avid barbecuers, and our neighbors have gotten used to the sight of us huddled over the barbecue, holding an umbrella to shield us from pouring rain, or bundled up in parkas and mitts in driving snow, intent on grilling kabobs. However, in the depths of winter, with a blizzard raging outside, even we are forced to abandon our barbecue. At such times, I adapt our favorite recipes to indoor cooking.

Modifying the recipes in this book for indoor preparation is simple. Instead of grilling the food on an outdoor barbecue, you can use a stove-top or electric grill. Failing that, you can use the broiler in your oven. You can also shallow fry the food instead of grilling it, or sauté it lightly. For making soups and chutneys, try boiling the ingredients instead of grilling them. For raitas and salads, use raw instead of grilled ingredients. Once you become familiar with Indian and tandoori cooking, you will find it easy to select the right cooking method for each recipe.

Please note that if you are using a gas grill, the temperature will rise quickly; if you have a charcoal grill, it will tend to heat more slowly but maintain the heat longer.

Though I enjoy cooking in all its forms, it is barbecuing that I love best. I love poking at the food as it grills. I love the smell of the food roasting and of the marinade as it hits the hot coals. I love listening to the meat hiss and sizzle. Above all, I love to watch the faces of my family and friends when they first taste the food.

This book is the result of years of experimentation. You will find many dishes that may be familiar to you from Indian restaurants; others are traditional and not usually cooked on the grill. I have tried to represent the cooking styles of the different regions of India to give you a culinary tour of the country. Some are my own creations, inspired by dishes that I have eaten during my travels. I have tried to make this book fun for both the cook and the people who taste the results. I hope cooking from it brings you as much pleasure as writing it brought me.

Namaskaar!

getting prepared

this section will help you decide exactly what supplies you need in your kitchen before preparing recipes from this book. It will also help identify unfamiliar spices and ingredients, and suggest where to buy supplies. If you have trouble finding any of these ingredients in your area, many are available by mail order from Kalustyan's, 123 Lexington Avenue, New York, NY 10016, tel. (212) 685–3451, fax (212) 683–8458.

Spices

Spices are an essential part of Indian cooking. They are used in many combinations and are often ground fresh for each use. Various techniques—such as frying, sautéing, roasting, powdering, or soaking the spice in vinegar, yogurt, or lemon juice—are employed to get the best out of each spice, often extracting different flavors from the same spice. In some cases, I use the same spice three different ways in a single recipe. In the yogurt marinade, for example, cumin seeds may be used whole, roasted and ground, or fried lightly in oil. In other dishes, I highlight just one spice, such as cardamom seeds. Your aim in spicing is to use the right combination and proportion of spices to enhance the flavor of the main ingredient without overpowering it. Spices are also used judiciously in cooking to help the body digest the food and heal itself.

Spices are best bought in small quantities and stored in airtight containers to retain their freshness. Whenever possible, buy whole spices and grind small amounts when needed. Store all your spices in a cool dark place.

Black Pepper
(*kali mirch*)

I use black pepper in almost every recipe, as I find that its aroma intensifies while grilling and brings out the flavor of the marinade. Whenever possible, use freshly ground black pepper. You can powder a small amount and keep it in an airtight container.

Black Salt
(*kala namak*)

You can find this only in Indian grocery stores, and it cannot be used in place of white table salt. Contrary to its name, powdered black salt is salmon pink in color. It is available in lumps or as a powder. Lumps are more flavorful and can be powdered when needed, though the powder is, of course, easier to use. It is usually paired with roasted ground cumin seeds to produce a distinctive flavor and aroma, and is an important spice in raitas, salads, and chutneys.

Cardamom
(*elaichi*)

Green cardamom is the most common variety used in this book. This spice is small, with a light green peel and a strong aroma. Cardamom can be found in all grocery stores, and you can also buy peeled cardamom. I recommend that you buy the whole cardamom and seed it if required; it stays fresh and holds its aroma longer. It is essential for making *garam masala* (a blend of spices) and can be ground, peel and all. In some of the recipes, I use black cardamom, which is readily available in Indian grocery stores. Black cardamom is bigger than the green variety and has a milder aroma. If you are unable to find any, you may substitute green for black cardamom.

Carom Seeds
(ajwain)

These tiny seeds taste a bit like thyme and have a very strong flavor. They are available only in Indian grocery stores and are used whole in this book.

Cayenne Pepper
(lal mirch)

Also known as chili powder, cayenne pepper is made from powdered dried hot red chilies. It is extremely hot, and care must be taken not to handle it directly with fingers or to touch the face and eyes. I have used very small amounts of cayenne pepper in each recipe; you can adjust the amounts to taste.

Chilies, green
(hari mirch)

I use small green chilies, but you can substitute jalapeño peppers or any other pepper of your choice. If you find them too hot, you can deseed them or use only half. Chilies are widely available in grocery stores.

Cinnamon
(dalchini)

Cinnamon can be bought in any grocery store in powder, chip, or stick form. I like to lightly fry stick cinnamon in oil, which infuses the food cooked in it with its aroma. It is also an important ingredient in making garam masala.

Cloves
(*lavang*)

Cloves are available in all grocery stores and are used in Indian cooking in whole or powder form. They are an essential component of garam masala and are also lightly fried in hot oil, which perfumes food that is to be cooked in it.

Coriander Seeds, ground
(*sookha dhaniya*)

Ground coriander seeds are an integral part of Indian cooking and are used in almost every recipe in this book. Although they are available both whole and powdered, it is best to buy them powdered in small amounts and keep them in airtight containers, as they lose their flavor with age.

Cumin Seeds, whole and ground
(*jeera, sabut aur pisa*)

Cumin seeds are the best-known and most widely used spice in Indian cooking. Cumin can be bought in any grocery store, whole or ground. Whole seeds are roasted and ground for use in *raitas* (yogurt relish) and chutneys.

Fennel Seeds
(*saunf*)

Fennel seeds are very similar to anise seeds in flavor and appearance. They have a sweet taste not unlike licorice. In this book, I use both whole and ground fennel seeds. You can buy them whole and powder them in small amounts in a clean coffee or spice grinder.

Fenugreek Seeds
(*methi*)

This bitter spice is used in small quantities. It is usually used whole and sometimes lightly fried in oil to bring out its strong aroma. Fenugreek seeds mellow and release their fragrance as they cook.

Garam Masala

Strangely enough, though this spice blend is crucial to northern Indian and Moghlai cooking, it has no English name. It is a fragrant mixture of cinnamon, cardamom, cloves, cumin seeds, and black pepper. A little bit of garam masala goes a long way, and it is usually added toward the end of cooking to preserve its fragrance. Although garam masala is sold in Indian grocery stores, I find that generally too much coriander and fenugreek are added as fillers, and the mixture loses its zesty quality. Good-quality garam masala can easily be made at home in a spice or coffee grinder.

Mustard Seeds
(*rai*)

These tiny, dark brown seeds are important in southern Indian cooking. They are usually lightly fried in hot oil before they are used; in Bengali cooking they are ground to a pungent paste. They are available at Indian and other grocery stores.

Onion Seeds
(*kalonji*)

Though the correct name for *kalonji* is nigella seeds, Indian stores call them onion seeds, so I have referred to them throughout the book as onion seeds. They are black and have an onion-like flavor that is also similar to oregano. They are available in Indian grocery stores and are usually used whole in Indian cooking.

Other Ingredients

Basmati Rice
(*basmati chaval*)

A variety of long-grained rice, basmati is generally reserved for special occasions. It has long slender grains and a delicious, nutty aroma. I recommend you use basmati rice for making *pulaos* (rice to which meat or vegetables have been added) and *biryanis* (a meat or chicken curry layered with rice). Basmati rice can now be found in all grocery stores.

Chickpea Flour
(*besan*)

Also known as gram flour, chickpea flour is made of dried and ground chickpeas. It is used to make batters for deep-fried *pakoras* (dumplings), and to thicken marinades and add crispness to tandoori preparations. It is pale yellow in color and should be stored in an airtight container to keep it fresh. It can be bought at Indian grocery stores.

Coconut Milk
(*nariyal ka doodh*)

Excellent canned coconut milk can be bought at all grocery stores. It is rich, creamy, and fresh tasting. Because making coconut milk at home is a laborious process, canned coconut milk offers a great substitute.

Mango, green cooking
(*hara aam*)

Cooking mangoes are different from the ripe ones available in summer. They can be bought year-round in Indian or Chinese grocery stores. They are very sour in flavor and add a nice tang to recipes. Raw mangoes are used in making chutneys and pickles. I also like to intersperse them with chicken or lamb on skewers.

Tamarind
(*imli*)

Ripe tamarind is chocolate brown in color and is sold peeled and seeded in small rectangular slabs in Indian grocery stores. Tamarind paste is also available in jars and is much easier to use. I find that the seeded tamarind has a richer flavor than the paste and prefer using it in spite of the bit of extra work involved. Soak it in hot water for at least an hour and pass it through a sieve to obtain the extract. If you are in a hurry, you can also microwave the soaked tamarind, liquid and all, for 1-2 minutes uncovered. Mash it with a fork and proceed as described in the recipe.

Herbs

Coriander, fresh
(*hara dhaniya*)

Also known as cilantro or Chinese parsley, this herb is abundant in all grocery stores. It is very fragrant and is used as a garnish, in chutneys and in sauces. The tender upper stems of the plant are also very flavorful and should not be discarded. Throw away only the root and fibrous parts. To store fresh coriander, slice off and discard the roots, wrap the coriander lightly in paper towels and store it in a plastic bag, refrigerated, for up to 2 weeks.

Curry Leaves
(*karipatta*)

Fresh curry leaves are extremely fragrant and are used in most southern Indian cooking. Curry leaves are thrown into hot oil with mustard seeds to lend a distinctive flavor to the food. They are also ground into chutneys and used in marinades. Fresh curry leaves are found in Indian grocery stores and can be refrigerated in plastic bags for 2 weeks. Use dried curry leaves only if you are unable to find them fresh, as they lose most of their flavor when dried.

Fenugreek Leaves, dried
(*kasoori methi*)

I frequently use dried fenugreek leaves because I find that their aroma is heightened during grilling, imbuing the food with a special scent. They are easily available at all Indian grocery stores and have an indefinite shelf life.

Mint, fresh and dried
(*podhina, taza aur sookha*)

Fresh mint is sold in all grocery stores and farmers' markets. It is used in making chutneys and in flavoring drinks and raitas. Fresh mint can be wrapped in paper towels and stored in plastic bags in the refrigerator for 2 weeks. Although dried mint leaves are available in Indian grocery stores, they are not as aromatic as those dried at home, which is easy to do with a microwave oven. Wash and dry the leaves, then microwave them on a plate lined with paper towels on high for 1 minute. Stir the mint around to turn the leaves and microwave again for 1 minute. Leave the plate out overnight, and the leaves should be dry and brittle the next morning.

Instead of microwaving them, you can also leave the leaves to dry on a plate on your kitchen counter for 3 days. You can store them indefinitely in an airtight container. Just crumble the leaves and blend them into recipes as required.

Appliances and Tools

Electric Coffee Grinder

Many of the spices used in this book can be bought ground from Indian grocery stores. However, some recipes call for making up a special, freshly ground spice mixture, which can be done with an electric coffee grinder. If you buy whole spices to powder in small amounts, or want to make your own garam masala or ground roasted cumin seeds, you will need this appliance. Electric coffee grinders are reasonably priced; you should keep one for spice-grinding only.

Food Processor or Blender

Either a food processor or blender is necessary to prepare marinades and grind meats. Lacking either one, chop the ingredients very finely instead of mincing, or grate them with a hand grater.

Skewers

I prefer using bamboo skewers, available everywhere, for my grilling. I don't find it necessary to soak them in cold water beforehand; they won't burn and fall off the grill. Skewer the food right from the top, leaving a little space at the end for the skewer to protrude from the barbecue's lid.

Some Cooking Techniques

Cottage Cheese
(*paneer*)

Cottage cheese is available in Indian and in some other grocery stores, and can be made at home. American cottage cheese is soft, uncompressed, and watery. Indian cottage cheese can be bought in rectangular blocks and can be cubed as it is compressed to drain all liquid. Freeze extra servings for later use.

2 quarts whole milk

2-3 tablespoons lemon juice

Bring the milk to a boil in a heavy-bottomed pan. Add the lemon juice and stir frequently until the curds separate from the milk, adding more lemon juice if needed. The curds will rise to the top, leaving behind a clear liquid. Line a fine sieve with two layers of cheesecloth and pour the curdled milk through it. Tie the ends of the cheesecloth together and hang the pouch to drain from the kitchen faucet. After half an hour, remove the cheese from the cloth and put it on a chopping board. Shape it into a ½-inch-thick square. Place a heavy weight over the cheese, such as a large pot filled with water, and leave the cheese for 3 to 4 hours. This will drain and compress the cheese. The paneer is now ready for use and can be stored, covered tightly with plastic wrap.

Dry-roasting Spices

This is a technique I use to intensify the flavor and aroma of spices. Warm a heavy-bottomed skillet (a nonstick skillet will do) over medium-low heat. Add the spices and stir for a few minutes. They should turn a few shades darker and emit their unique roasted aroma. Remove the pan from the stove and let the spices cool before powdering them. You can also roast and powder small batches of cumin seeds this way. Store in an airtight container.

Garam Masala

Garam masala is indispensable in Indian cooking. It can be bought in Indian grocery stores, though I find the quality inferior. You can easily make garam masala at home with an electric coffee grinder, in batches big enough to last 3 to 4 months.

1½ tablespoons green
   cardamom pods

4 1-inch sticks of
   cinnamon

1 tablespoon whole
   cloves

1 teaspoon whole
   black pepper

1 teaspoon cumin
   seeds

**MAKES ABOUT 4
TABLESPOONS**

Put all the spices in a clean coffee grinder and grind to a fine powder. Transfer to an airtight container and store in a cool dry place.

indian grill

appetizers and drinks

guchchi masaledaar *Grilled mushrooms marinated in spices, lemon juice, and fresh coriander* **bhuna hua bhutta** *Roasted buttered corn with salt and lemon juice* **bhuni sabzi milwan** *Mixed vegetables marinated in spicy oil and lemon juice* **bhune hue papad** *Grilled pappadums* **dhaniya murgh tikka** *Chicken breast marinated in fresh coriander, ginger, and lemon juice* **lal murgh** *Chicken breast marinated in a paste of sweet red peppers, onion, and spices* **karara jhinga** *Crispy shrimp marinated with chickpea flour, eggs, and sour cream* **bhune tamatar ka ras** *Juice of roasted tomatoes with cumin and Tabasco* **panna** *Roasted green mango juice* **majhige** *Roasted garlic in spicy yogurt*

*W*hen the doorbell rings in the evening, I catch myself doing a quick mental inventory of the snacks I have on hand. This is a conditioned reflex I developed in India that lingers with me even after all these years of living outside the country. Indians love to socialize, and one of the cardinal rules of hospitality is that any guest entering the house be plied with food and drink. Calling ahead to inform the hosts that you are planning to visit them would be considered absurdly formal by most Indians. My mother's theory is that by not telling your hosts you are coming, you spare them having to make elaborate preparations. Every Indian hostess (and it is usually the hostess; most Indian men are lamentably unconcerned with these details) keeps a large stock of snacks handy, prepared for every eventuality. The mark of a good hostess is how lavish a spread she can produce on short notice. If she has cooked it all, so much the better; store-bought is considered inferior. If you see a kid running out the back door to the nearest shop as you enter from the front, it is not a good sign!

Appetizers are always accompanied by drinks. The first question is always "*thanda* or *garam*?"—literally, "hot or cold?" In northern India, hot inevitably means tea with milk and sugar, sometimes with ginger and cardamom. Tea drinkers will assure you that a cup of hot tea will cool you down in summer and keep you warm in winter—I've never figured out how! If you pick cold, you can choose from a huge repertoire of chilled drinks known as *sherbat* (from which the English word sherbet is derived) made from fruits, sugar, nuts, and spices. My grandmother bottled juice concentrates in the summer months that could be diluted with ice and served to guests.

In this section, you will find a wide selection of appetizers that can double as side dishes. All the recipes cook quickly, so you can pass them around while the rest of the meal is cooking. Leftovers are useful ingredients for salads or light lunches when wrapped in a tortilla and topped with chopped tomatoes or shredded lettuce. If you have more than one type of leftover appetizer on hand, combine them and create an intriguing new dish! I have designed each dish to serve between two to six people, but you can easily halve or double the recipe according to your needs.

guchchi masaledaar

Grilled mushrooms marinated with spices, lemon juice,
and fresh coriander

Mushrooms are a relatively new addition to Indian cuisine. When I was young, you could only find them in some gourmet food shops in Delhi and Bombay, and whenever my father traveled to these cities he would bring back a big bag of white button mushrooms. Together we would pore over cookbooks to find recipes for their use. I find that mushrooms are particularly suited for grilling because they remain moist inside and acquire a nice char outside. This is a useful appetizer to have on hand because it cooks quickly and people can munch on it while the rest of the food is cooking. You can also serve it as a side dish.

3 cloves of garlic, peeled

1 -inch piece of ginger, peeled

½ cup packed fresh coriander leaves and tender upper stems, washed and drained

¼ cup lemon juice

Salt to taste

¼–½ teaspoon ground black pepper

½ teaspoon roasted ground cumin seeds

½ teaspoon garam masala

¼ cup olive oil

1 lb. white mushrooms, washed and drained

SERVES 4

Mince all ingredients except the mushrooms in a food processor or blender until well blended, then transfer the contents to a mixing bowl. Toss in the mushrooms and coat well with the marinade. Cover and keep at room temperature for 1 hour. When ready to grill, lift the mushrooms out of the marinade, and thread them onto skewers. Place the skewers in a covered medium-hot grill. Grill for about 5 minutes, then flip the skewers to cook the mushrooms on the other side for about 5 minutes. Do not overcook; just let them brown lightly. To check doneness, slice a mushroom in half. If it is moist (and not drying up), uncover the lid, turn up the heat, and lightly char them for another 2 minutes. To serve, slide the mushrooms off the skewers and drop them back into the leftover marinade. Toss once again to coat and serve hot.

bhuna hua bhutta

Roasted buttered corn with salt and lemon juice

India's city streets are dotted with vendors selling roasted corn from pushcarts, which are equipped with portable charcoal grills where the corn is roasted while you wait. It is usually grilled without any butter, the only condiment being a rub of lemon juice and salt applied after the corn is done. I find grilled corn makes a delicious appetizer, and it is especially popular with children, who are liable to make it a complete meal.

4 ears of fresh corn, shucked

4 tablespoons of melted butter for basting

Salt to taste

Lemon juice

SERVES 4

Place the corn directly on a barbecue grill. Cover and roast on medium heat, occasionally basting with butter and turning the cobs to ensure even cooking. When the corn smells roasted and is charred in some spots and lightly browned in others, it is done. This should take about 15 minutes. Remove to a platter. Sprinkle all the cobs with salt and lemon juice to taste, and serve hot.

bhuni sabzi milwan

Mixed vegetables marinated in spicy oil and lemon juice

A medley of spices is used in the marinade of this appetizer to create a very aromatic dish. Roasting the spices before powdering them intensifies their flavor. You can also serve these vegetables as a side dish and convert any leftovers into a hearty soup, such as Mili Juli Sabzi ka Shorva (grilled mixed vegetable soup in chicken broth, page 25).

½ teaspoon fenugreek seeds

½ teaspoon cumin seeds

½ teaspoon coriander seeds

½ teaspoon fennel seeds

¼ teaspoon whole black pepper

2 cardamom, peeled and seeded, or seeds from 2 cardamom

2 cloves of garlic, peeled

½ -inch piece of ginger, peeled

1 hot green chili

½ cup packed fresh coriander leaves and tender upper stems, washed and drained

¼ cup lemon juice

¼ cup olive oil

Salt to taste

6 large white mushrooms

2 medium ripe tomatoes, halved

1 medium sweet red pepper, halved lengthwise

1 medium sweet green pepper, halved lengthwise

1 medium zucchini, halved lengthwise

1 small eggplant, halved lengthwise

1 medium red onion, peeled and halved

SERVES 4 TO 6

Place a skillet over medium heat and dry roast the fenugreek seeds, cumin seeds, coriander seeds, fennel seeds, black pepper, and cardamom seeds. You can roast them all together until they smell roasted and turn a few shades darker (this will only take a few minutes). Cool and finely powder them in a spice or coffee grinder and set aside. In a blender or food processor, combine the garlic, ginger, green chili, fresh coriander, lemon juice, olive oil, and salt. Blend as smoothly as possible. Transfer to a large mixing bowl and add the powdered spices. Mix well. Put the mushrooms in the marinade and roll them around a bit to coat. Remove and place on a large platter. Now brush or spoon the marinade onto the vegetables, or roll them around in the marinade until well coated. Remove to the platter. Heat the barbecue to medium high and place all the vegetables on the open grill, turning for evenness until just charred. The mushrooms will be the first to come off the grill, in about 8 to 10 minutes. The tomatoes should be done next in 12 to 15 minutes, and so on. Remove to the platter as each vegetable is done. Slice the zucchini and eggplant, halve the mushrooms, and halve each half of the onion and tomatoes. Seed and stem the peppers, then slice. Throw all the vegetables and their juices back into the bowl with the remaining marinade, toss gently to mix and serve hot.

bhune hue papad

Grilled pappadums

Pappadums are a familiar sight to anyone who has eaten at Indian restaurants, where they are frequently served as appetizers. They are dried, paper-thin disks made from highly seasoned lentil paste. Pappadums are usually deep-fried, which leaves them somewhat greasy. With the barbecue grill, however, you can make perfect pappadums without using any oil or butter. As a fat-free snack or appetizer, they are hard to beat. They roast very quickly and are handy for guests to nibble on while the rest of the food is being barbecued.

6 assorted pappadums, such as cumin seed or black pepper (readily available at Indian groceries or by mail order)

SERVES 4

Have a grill ready on medium-high heat. Grill each pappadum individually, using tongs, until little bubbles appear on the surface and it changes color from pale yellow to golden or darker yellow, which will take only a few seconds. Repeat on the other side.

dhaniya murgh tikka

Chicken breast marinated in fresh coriander, ginger, and lemon juice

Fresh coriander is an herb used extensively in Indian cooking. It is often the main ingredient in chutneys; it is also used as a garnish or, as in the following recipe, a marinade. *Tikkas* are pieces of boned meat marinated in spices and grilled. These tikkas, imbued with the smell of charcoal and perfumed with the fragrance of fresh coriander, are a great start to any meal. Have a bowl of Mint Yogurt Dip (page 50) or Khatti Meethi Tamatar ki Chatni (sweet, sour, and spicy tomato chutney with ginger, page 45) on the side for people to dunk their tikkas in.

1 medium onion, peeled and coarsely chopped

1 -inch piece of ginger, peeled and coarsely chopped

1 cup tightly packed fresh coriander leaves and tender upper stems, washed and drained

Salt to taste

¼–½ teaspoon ground black pepper

½ teaspoon ground coriander seeds

½ teaspoon ground cumin seeds

½ teaspoon garam masala

¼ cup lemon juice

1 lb. boneless, skinless chicken breast, cut into 1-inch pieces, washed and dried

SERVES 4

Mince the onion and ginger in a food processor or blender. Add the coriander and mince again; then add the salt, pepper, ground coriander, ground cumin, garam masala, and lemon juice and mince again. Transfer to a bowl, add the chicken and toss well to coat. Cover and refrigerate for no longer than 2 hours. When ready to barbecue, thread the chicken pieces onto skewers, leaving a little space in between. Place on a medium-hot barbecue, cover and cook for about 8 minutes per side. Baste with leftover marinade and turn occasionally for even cooking. Now remove the cover of the grill, turn up the heat, and char lightly for a few minutes more. To serve, slide off skewers and heap onto a plate.

lal murgh

Chicken breast marinated in a paste of sweet red peppers, onion, and spices

This recipe employs an unusual marinade: minced sweet red peppers. When the marinated chicken grills, the distinctive aroma is of these peppers. You can arrange the chicken on a bed of lettuce for a pretty contrast of colors. If you do not wish to serve the chicken as an appetizer, it can be used as a side dish and served along with Saag Seekh Kabob (skewered lamb kabobs ground with spinach and spices, page 88) or Chatniwale Seekh Kabob (skewers of ground lamb marinated with fresh herbs, page 90), naan (a traditional leavened bread), and a tomato chutney. Leftovers can be stuffed into pita bread and topped with a little raita (yogurt relish).

1 medium onion, peeled and coarsely chopped

4 cloves of garlic, peeled and coarsely chopped

1 -inch piece of ginger, peeled and coarsely chopped

1 medium sweet red pepper, seeded, stemmed, and coarsely chopped

½ teaspoon garam masala

½ teaspoon ground cumin seeds

½ teaspoon ground coriander seeds

Salt to taste

¼–½ teaspoon ground black pepper

2 tablespoons plain yogurt

1 lb. boneless, skinless chicken breast, cut into 1-inch chunks, washed and dried

Lemon juice

SERVES 4

Mince the onion, garlic, ginger, and red pepper in a food processor or blender. Add all the spices and yogurt and mince again. Transfer to a bowl and add the chicken. Toss to mix, cover and refrigerate for 4 hours or longer. When ready to grill, lift the chicken out of the marinade and thread onto skewers. Cook covered on a medium-hot grill, turning occasionally until tender and lightly browned, about 8 minutes per side. Spoon some of the leftover marinade over the skewers as they cook. When the chicken is done, uncover, turn up the heat and char the skewers slightly for a few minutes more. Slide chicken off the skewers, heap onto a platter, and sprinkle with lemon juice.

karara Jhinga

Crispy shrimp marinated with chickpea flour, eggs, and sour cream

As a child, when I visited Goa I would often go down to the beach with my brothers to watch the fishermen bring in the day's catch of shrimp. A lot of the shrimp were cooked right there on the beach in little shacks, where they were barbecued and served hot off the grill. Even today, the heady aroma of shrimp grilling on a barbecue brings back vivid memories of those delightful flavors. Shrimps are abundant in India's coastal areas such as Goa, Kerala, and Orissa, and are cooked in many different ways. In Goa they may be cooked in vinegar and spices, in Kerala with coconut and curry leaves, and in the North with yogurt and garam masala. In this recipe the shrimp are marinated in a spicy batter with the unusual addition of eggs and chickpea flour (besan), which make them quite crispy when barbecued. Karara Jhinga goes exceptionally well with Khatti Meethi Tamatar ki Chatni (sweet, sour, and spicy tomato chutney with ginger, page 45) or with Jhatpat Tamatar wali Chatni (grilled tomato salsa, page 46).

¼ -inch piece of ginger, peeled and grated

2 cloves of garlic, peeled and grated

1 large egg

2 tablespoons sour cream

2 tablespoons chickpea flour (besan)

Salt to taste

½ teaspoon ground black pepper

¼ teaspoon garam masala

¼ teaspoon ground cumin seeds

¼ teaspoon ground coriander seeds

½ lb. uncooked shrimp, fresh or frozen, peeled, deveined, and washed

Lemon juice

SERVES 2

Combine the ginger, garlic, and egg in a mixing bowl and beat lightly. Add the sour cream and mix again. Add the chickpea flour and all the remaining ingredients except the lemon juice and mix well. Toss in the shrimp and coat well with the marinade. Cover and refrigerate for at least 1 hour. When ready to grill, lift the shrimp out of the marinade and thread onto skewers, leaving a little gap in between. Cook on an open barbecue on medium-high heat and coat occasionally with the marinade, taking care not to let the shrimp burn. Cook for about 5 to 7 minutes on each side, making sure that the marinade, as well as the shrimp, gets cooked. When lightly browned and crisp, remove skewers from the grill and serve with a generous sprinkling of lemon juice.

bhune tamatar ka ras

Juice of roasted tomatoes with cumin and Tabasco

This recipe is from my mother's repertoire and brings back vivid childhood recollections of picking ripe tomatoes from her huge vegetable garden and watching her make jugs of this juice to keep in the refrigerator during summertime. All of us found its fresh tangy taste ideal for keeping the Delhi heat at bay. This juice is best made in late summer when vine-ripened tomatoes are plentiful and the taste of the sun can be savored in the drink. You can also serve it as chilled soup with chopped cucumbers, sweet green and red peppers, and celery mixed in.

1 lb. ripe tomatoes (about 3-4 medium)

½ cup water

1 tablespoon sugar

Salt to taste

¼ teaspoon ground black pepper

¼ teaspoon roasted ground cumin seeds

A generous dash of Tabasco sauce

SERVES 2

Wrap each tomato in foil and place on a covered grill on medium-low heat for about 20 minutes. The tomatoes should be mushy and smell roasted when they are done. Cool and peel them, reserving any liquid left in the foil cup. Put the tomatoes in a blender and add all the remaining ingredients. Blend until smooth. Strain the juice to remove the seeds and serve chilled.

p̄anna

Roasted green mango juice

Panna in Hindi means emerald, which is an enchanting description of the delicate green color of this juice. It is often served along with the main meal to temper the spiciness of the food. In the hot summer months, every home keeps a cooling jug of panna because it is supposed to prevent heat stroke, always a concern in the hot climate. Typically panna is made by burying mangoes in glowing charcoal until roasted and then extracting the juice. To roast the mangoes on a charcoal grill, wrap the mangoes in some foil and place them directly over low-burning coals; if using a gas barbecue, place the mangoes unwrapped on the grill. Because the mangoes take some time to soften, I usually put them on the grill at the end of a cookout, to be used for a later meal. I find that the sweet-and-sour, mildly spicy taste of panna is very refreshing before a meal.

3 unripe green cooking mangoes (1½ lb.)

4 cups water

½ cup sugar

½ teaspoon salt

½ teaspoon black salt (optional)

½ teaspoon roasted ground cumin seeds

1 teaspoon dried mint leaves *or* 1 tablespoon chopped fresh mint leaves

1 teaspoon fresh grated ginger

SERVES 4

Grill the mangoes, covered, on medium heat for about 20 to 30 minutes, until softened. Turn occasionally to cook evenly. Cool and peel, scraping off and saving all the pulp attached to the skins. Immerse the peeled mangoes and the pulp in the water and squeeze out all the pulp sticking to the seeds. Discard the seeds. Add the rest of the ingredients to the mango juice and mix well. You may wish to strain the juice before serving, although this is not usually done in India. Serve chilled.

majhige

Roasted garlic in spicy yogurt

In the southern state of Karnataka, Majhige is served along with meals to soothe the taste buds after a dose of spicy curries. It is usually made quite thin, tart, and mildly spicy. Although the garlic is not traditionally roasted before being added to Majhige, its charbroiled aroma and mild taste add a nice flavor to the drink. When I was living in a college dorm in Bangalore, our cook often served it for dinner and it was the major attraction of the meal.

2 large cloves of garlic, peeled

1 cup plain yogurt

1 cup water

Salt to taste

1 tablespoon lemon juice

1 tablespoon vegetable oil

½ teaspoon black mustard seeds

1 hot green chili, finely chopped

8–10 chopped curry leaves, preferably fresh

1 tablespoon chopped fresh coriander leaves

SERVES 2

Wrap the cloves of garlic in foil and place on a medium-hot grill. Cover and roast for about 8 minutes. The cloves should be lightly charred and softened when they are done. Cool and chop as finely as you can or mash with a fork. In a bowl, beat the yogurt with a spoon for a few minutes until smooth. Add the water, salt, lemon juice, and the chopped garlic. Mix well. Heat the oil in a small pan or butter warmer over medium-high heat and add the mustard seeds. As soon as they begin to splutter, add the green chili and the curry leaves. Sauté for about 1 minute, or until everything is evenly fried. Then pour the spiced oil into the yogurt, along with the fresh coriander leaves. Mix gently and serve at room temperature.

Soups and Salads

kalan mullagatanni *Grilled mushrooms served in a roasted tomato tamarind broth with black pepper* **bhune tamatar ka shorva** *Roasted-tomato soup with cumin and fresh coriander* **Cholam Soop** *Grilled corn and onion soup in a coconut and cream broth* **Rasam** *Spicy grilled tomato soup* **mili juli sabzi ka shorva** *Grilled mixed vegetable soup in chicken broth* **kaddoo ka shorva** *Grilled pumpkin soup with cream and scallions* **tandoori murgh salat** *Grilled chicken salad with tomatoes and green onions in a spicy yogurt dressing* **bhutte ka salat** *Grilled corn and roasted red peppers tossed with onions in a lemon and roasted-spice dressing* **hare aam aur bundgobhi ka salat** *Grilled scallops and green mangoes tossed with shredded cabbage and red onion in a mustard lemon dressing* **Shakarkandi ki Chaat** *Sweet potatoes tossed with spices and lemon juice* **Jhinge aur simla mirch ka salat** *Shrimp and roasted red pepper salad with a sour cream, honey, and lime dressing* **salat-e-kabob** *Grilled ground meat kabobs tossed in a thickened yogurt, mint, and coriander dressing*

i like to serve dinner the traditional Indian way, by placing all the dishes on the table at once rather than serving individual courses. The concept of eating soup as a separate course was unknown to Indians until the British arrived. The closest thing to soup Indians had was *rasam*, which is made from tomatoes and black pepper and eaten with rice. When the British insisted on a separate soup course, their Indian cooks resorted to serving rasam, dressed up with a little broth and bits of meat, and the famous mulligatawny soup was born. In recent years, with many more Indians traveling abroad and bringing back Western influences, it has become quite fashionable to serve soup. Creative cooks have devised many recipes using Indian ingredients and spices that appeal to Indian palates.

In this chapter you will find recipes for soups made from grilled ingredients. Some are traditional family recipes, and others are my own creations. Some of the soups are light and make excellent starters to a meal, while others stand alone. I suggest grilling the ingredients in advance, possibly at the tail end of another barbecue. They can keep refrigerated for up to a week until needed. If all the ingredients are on hand, soup is very easy to put together on short notice.

Restaurant menus that offer only soup and salad for lunch would baffle most Indians, who cannot fathom salad as the mainstay of any meal. Traditional Indian salads are simple platters of sliced cucumbers or tomatoes, or a melange of chopped onions, cucumbers, tomatoes, and radishes tossed with lemon juice and roasted ground cumin seeds. The purpose of salads in an Indian meal is to soothe the palate after the spiciness of the food and to add a refreshing crunch to the meal. It is always a part of the main meal, never a meal by itself. When I was working out recipes for grilled salads I had Western readers in mind, so you will find that many of the dishes are substantial enough for a complete lunch or dinner. Some of the salads can be effortlessly made if you have any leftover pieces of grilled meat, chicken, or seafood. Give free rein to your imagination in substituting ingredients. The dressings can also be made ahead of time and refrigerated for up to 3 days.

kalan mullagatanni

Grilled mushrooms served in a roasted tomato-tamarind broth with black pepper

"Mulligatawny" soup has become such a familiar part of English cuisine that few people are aware of its Indian origins. Along with curry powder and Major Grey's chutneys, it is one of the most enduring relics of the British Raj in India. Legend has it that the English were so fond of this soup that they would carry back bottles of it to Britain, where it quickly became popular. The word itself is derived from two Tamil words: *mullaga*, meaning pepper, and *tanni*, meaning water. In other words, pepper water. As the name suggests, the soup is very hot and only the brave should try the traditional version. The recipe given here is a slight variation of the original one. I have added grilled mushrooms to the soup, which impart a nice meatiness to the taste. Also, roasting the tomatoes before puréeing them gives a charred aroma to the soup. The amount of pepper can be adjusted according to your level of daring. The soup makes a delicious lunch served with a crusty bread and a salad on the side.

1 lb. red ripe tomatoes (about 3–4 medium)

Salt to taste

¼ teaspoon ground black pepper

¼ cup olive oil

1 lb. large white mushrooms, washed and drained

A lime-sized piece of seedless tamarind (4 oz.), soaked in ½ cup hot water for at least 1 hour

2 tablespoons vegetable oil

¼ teaspoon black mustard seeds

5–6 curry leaves, preferably fresh

1 small onion, peeled and finely chopped

Salt to taste

½ teaspoon freshly cracked black pepper

¼ teaspoon turmeric

1 cup water

SERVES 2

Wrap the tomatoes individually in foil and grill, covered, on low heat for about 20 minutes or until they are soft and smell roasted. Meanwhile, mix the salt and ¼ teaspoon black pepper into the olive oil and add the mushrooms. Toss to coat. When the tomatoes are done, thread the mushrooms onto skewers and grill, covered, on medium heat for about 5 minutes on each side. Throw them back into the marinade. When the tomatoes are cool enough to handle, transfer to a bowl along with any accumulated liquid from their foil cups, and peel them. Mash them well with a fork and strain the liquid. Put the soaked tamarind in a sieve set over a bowl and squeeze out the pulp with your hands, discarding the fibers and seeds, if any. Mix the strained tamarind liquid into the strained tomato liquid.

Lift the mushrooms out of the bowl, reserving any accumulated liquid, and slice them thinly. In a skillet, heat the vegetable oil over a medium flame and add the mustard seeds and curry leaves. As soon as they begin to splutter, add the chopped onion. Sauté for 5 to 7 minutes, or until lightly browned. Add the sliced mushrooms to the onions. Sauté for 2 minutes, then add all the reserved mushroom liquid and the strained tomato-tamarind broth. Add the salt, freshly cracked black pepper, and the turmeric. Mix in 1 cup of water. Simmer for about 10 minutes on low heat, stirring occasionally.

bhune tamatar ka shorva

Roasted-tomato soup with cumin and fresh coriander

One of my favorites, this soup is easy to prepare and loaded with the rich flavor of vine-ripened tomatoes. As a child, I would ladle a generous helping of the soup into my bowl of rice and enjoy a most satisfying meal. To this day, rice and tomato soup ranks as my number one comfort food!

4 medium, ripe tomatoes (about 2 lbs.)

½ cup water

1 tablespoon butter

½ teaspoon cumin seeds

Salt to taste

¼ teaspoon ground black pepper

1 teaspoon sugar

1 tablespoon chopped fresh coriander leaves

SERVES 2

Wrap the tomatoes individually in foil and grill, covered, on medium-low heat for about 20 minutes, until cooked through and mushy. Cool to room temperature. Unwrap the tomatoes from the foil, reserving any accumulated liquid. Peel the tomatoes and mash with a fork. Add any juices reserved from the foil wrappings and pass through a sieve, discarding the seeds. You should have about 2½ cups of tomato juice left after straining the tomatoes. Add ½ cup of water and set aside. If you find that you have slightly less than 2½ cups of tomato juice, add more water to get three cups of liquid. Heat the butter over a medium flame. Add the cumin seeds. As soon as they start to splutter, add the tomato liquid, standing back as you do so, because it will spatter. Add salt, pepper, and sugar, and reduce heat to medium low. Cook for about 8 to 10 minutes and mix in the fresh coriander leaves just before serving.

Cholam Soop

Grilled corn and onion soup in a coconut and cream broth

Coconut milk is used extensively in southern Indian cooking to make curries and desserts. Preparing coconut milk at home is a laborious process. The coconut is first ground to a paste with water and then squeezed to extract the milk. Fortunately, American grocery stores stock excellent canned coconut milk. The recipe here uses coconut milk and cream for a broth which, combined with the corn, makes the soup deliciously sweet. Cholam Soop is mildly spiced to let the flavor of the grilled corn come through.

2 medium cobs of fresh sweet corn (such as peaches and cream), shucked

1 medium onion, peeled

1 tablespoon melted butter, for basting

2 tablespoons vegetable oil

½ teaspoon cumin seeds

1 cup canned coconut milk

1 cup water

Salt to taste

½ teaspoon ground black pepper

1 teaspoon sugar

½ cup half and half

SERVES 2 TO 4

Roast the corn and onion on a medium-hot grill, covered, for about 15 minutes. Baste the corn all over with the butter once and turn for even cooking. The corn and the onion should be charred in spots and smell roasted when done. Set aside to cool. With a sharp knife, remove the kernels from the corncob and chop the onion as finely as possible. In a skillet, heat oil over a medium flame and add the cumin seeds. After a second, add the corn and onion. Sauté for 2 minutes, then add the coconut milk and the water. Mix in the salt, pepper, and sugar. Cook, stirring now and then, for about 5 to 8 minutes. Turn off the heat, then mix in the half and half. Let the soup sit for 5 minutes before serving it. If you are planning to serve this soup later, warm it over gentle heat without letting it come to a boil.

Rasam

Spicy grilled tomato soup

Rasam is undoubtedly the most popular dish in southern India. It is served at every meal and is almost always eaten with rice. It typically forms part of the main meal rather than being served as soup at the beginning. In restaurants, rasam is served with vadas, deep-fried dumplings made from lentil batter, which soak up all the spiciness and flavor of the soup and add their own aroma and taste. When I was studying in Bangalore, I would often be invited to dine at friends' homes and got to eat some superb rasams, no two of which ever tasted the same. The recipe here was given to me by my friend Sandhya Murthy, who likes to serve the chunky version of this dish rather than the more common version made with strained tomato pulp.

SERVES 4

1 lb. ripe Italian plum tomatoes (about 6), halved

2 tablespoons vegetable oil

½ teaspoon black mustard seeds

¼ teaspoon cumin seeds

1 small onion, finely chopped

1 green chili, finely chopped

1 clove of garlic, finely chopped

10 curry leaves, fresh or dried, minced

A lime-sized piece of seedless tamarind (4 oz.), soaked in ½ cup hot water for at least 1 hour

1 cup water

½ teaspoon turmeric

Salt to taste

¼ teaspoon ground black pepper

¼ teaspoon ground cumin seeds

1 teaspoon sugar

2 tablespoons chopped fresh coriander leaves

On an open barbecue grill at medium heat, grill the tomatoes cut side up for about 10 minutes, turning them until lightly charred. Cool, then peel and quarter them. In a skillet, heat the oil over a medium-high flame. Add the mustard and cumin seeds. As soon as they begin to splutter, add the chopped onion, chili, garlic, and curry leaves. Sauté for about 5 minutes, or until the vegetables are lightly browned. While the onions are sautéing, set a sieve over a bowl and squeeze the soaked tamarind through, discarding the fibrous residue. Add the tamarind liquid to the pot along with 1 cup of water, turmeric, salt, pepper, ground cumin, and sugar. Stir to mix, then add the chopped tomatoes. Cook for about 5 minutes, then mix in the chopped fresh coriander leaves and serve hot.

mili juli sabzi ka shorva

Grilled mixed vegetable soup in chicken broth

This is a good way to use leftover grilled vegetables from the appetizer section (such as Bhuni Sabzi Milwan, chunks of mixed vegetables marinated in spicy oil and lemon juice, page 8)—a light, flavorful soup, excellent for a quick lunch or a light supper. You can also add cooked rice or noodles to the soup to make it heartier.

1 cup chicken broth

1 cup water

1 lb. grilled mixed vegetables (2¼ cups), using vegetables from

the Bhuni Sabzi Milwan (mixed vegetables grilled with spiced oil) recipe from the appetizer section

Salt to taste

SERVES 4

Mix the broth and the water in a pan and bring to a boil over medium-high heat. Reduce heat to low and add the vegetables and their juices.

Adjust the salt according to taste. Simmer the soup for about 10 minutes. Serve hot.

kaddoo ka shorva

Grilled pumpkin soup with cream and scallions

Pumpkins are cooked in many different ways in India: deep-fried and braised with sautéed onions and yogurt for a fancy dinner; mixed with yogurt to make a *raita* (yogurt relish) served especially at weddings; and cooked with milk, sugar, and cardamom to make a sumptuous dessert. Surprisingly, I had never tasted pumpkin soup until I came to America and had it at my friend Nina Bassuk's house. She makes a superb soup using sautéed onions and tomatoes with cream and scallions. Here is her recipe with a few additional spices for a more Indian flavor. A robust garlic bread and a salad would be perfect accompaniments.

1 lb. pumpkin, peeled and deseeded

1½ cups water

Salt to taste

½ teaspoon garam masala

6 tablespoons vegetable oil

¼ teaspoon fenugreek seeds

2 medium onions, peeled and finely chopped

2 medium tomatoes, chopped

1 cup chicken broth

½ cup heavy cream

2 tablespoons lemon juice

2 scallions (green onions), chopped (for garnish)

Fresh coriander leaves, chopped (for garnish)

SERVES 2

Scrape off and discard all the fiber from the peeled pumpkin. Cut it into 1-inch cubes. Wash cubes and put them in a microwave-safe bowl along with 1½ cups of water. Seal tightly with plastic wrap and microwave on high for 8 minutes. Drain and cool the pumpkin pieces. Mix the salt and garam masala with 3 tablespoons of the vegetable oil and then toss the pumpkin in. Coat well with the spiced oil and thread about 5 pieces onto a skewer. Place the skewers on a covered grill on medium-high heat. Cook until they are soft and are charred in spots, about 10 minutes. Flip the skewers to make sure the pumpkin chars all over. Slide the pieces back into the bowl they were marinating in and mash them with a fork until smooth. You should have about 1½ cups of pumpkin purée when you are done. In a skillet, heat the remaining oil over a medium-high flame and add the fenugreek seeds. After a few seconds, add the chopped onions. Sauté until the onions are lightly browned, about 5 to 7 minutes, then add the chopped tomatoes and cook for another 5 minutes, mashing them with the back of a spoon to soften them. Add the mashed pumpkin, more salt if desired, and chicken broth. Mix well and bring to a boil. Immediately turn off the heat and let the pan cool on the stove. When it is cool enough to handle, pass the soup through a sieve, squeezing with your hands or a spoon as you do so. Put the strained soup in a pan and heat it gently. Add the cream and lemon juice and remove from heat. Scatter the scallions and fresh coriander leaves over the soup. Adjust seasonings and add a dash more garam masala if you feel the soup needs it. Have some freshly ground black pepper at the table for extra spice.

tandoori murgh salat

Grilled chicken salad with tomatoes and green onions in a spicy yogurt dressing

This is a good salad to rustle up for a light lunch if you have just a couple of pieces of leftover barbecued chicken. Almost any grilled chicken recipe from this book would work well in this salad. You can serve it in many ways, too: rolled up in a warm pita bread or naan; stuffed in half of a pita pocket lined with crisp lettuce leaves; or sandwiched in a crusty roll.

2 tablespoons plain yogurt

Salt to taste

¼ teaspoon ground black pepper

¼ teaspoon roasted ground cumin seeds

¼ teaspoon garam masala

1 teaspoon lemon juice

2 pieces of leftover tandoori chicken (about 8 oz.), deboned and cut into bite-sized pieces

4 cherry tomatoes, halved, or 1 medium tomato, chopped

1 green onion with 2-inch stalk, thinly sliced

SERVES 2

In a bowl, beat the yogurt for a minute with a spoon to break up all the lumps. Add the salt, pepper, roasted cumin, garam masala, and lemon juice. Add the chicken and toss well to coat. Add the tomato and green onion to the chicken in the bowl, tossing gently to mix. Serve chilled or at room temperature.

bhutte ka salat

*Grilled corn and roasted red peppers tossed with onions
in a lemon and roasted-spice dressing*

In Indian cooking the flavor of any dish depends not only on the
spices that go into it but also on their preparation. Spices may be powdered,
roasted, fried, ground, boiled, or soaked in vinegar; each method extracts a different flavor from the same spice. Here, roasted coriander seeds and black cardamom are added to this salad dressing to make it aromatic and delicious. If you
do not have a black cardamom on hand, you may substitute a green one.

1 **large ear of fresh
corn, shucked**

1 **medium sweet
red pepper**

1 **teaspoon melted
butter, for
basting**

½ **red onion, finely
chopped**

Salt to taste

2 **tablespoons
lemon juice**

¼ **teaspoon cumin
seeds**

¼ **teaspoon whole
coriander seeds**

¼ **teaspoon whole
black pepper**

1 **black cardamom**

SERVES 4

Roast the corn and the red pepper,
covered, on medium-high heat for
about 15 minutes. Baste the corn all
over with the butter and roast until
lightly charred. Place the pepper in a
brown paper bag to cool for about 15

minutes. Let the corn cool to room temperature, then, using a sharp knife, cut
off the kernels. Peel away the charred skin from the pepper and wash the pepper under running water. Dry it, remove the stem and seeds, and chop into one-
inch pieces. In a bowl, toss the onion, corn kernels, and red pepper together. Add
the salt and lemon juice. Place a skillet on medium heat and add the whole
spices. Dry roast them for 2 to 3 minutes or until they darken and emit their
special roasted aroma. In a clean coffee or spice grinder, grind them to a powder. Add these powdered spices to the salad and mix well. This salad tastes best
warm or when served at room temperature.

hare aam aur bundgobhi ka salat

Grilled scallops and green mangoes tossed with shredded cabbage and red onion in a mustard lemon dressing

I have based this recipe on an unusual cabbage salad that I ate years ago at my friend Kiran's house in Bangalore. Here I have built on that recipe by adding a few more ingredients. The barbecued scallops add their own aroma and flavor to the dish, making it almost a meal by itself. All you might want is a loaf of crusty bread on the side or a tomato-based soup such as Kalan Mullagatanni (grilled mushrooms in tomato-tamarind broth, page 20) or Bhune Tamatar ka Shorva (roasted-tomato soup with cumin, page 22). This salad tastes best when it is served warm. You could, if you wish, substitute shrimp for the scallops. When choosing the green mango, try to find one that is just starting to ripen. Its sweet and sour flavors will blend well with the salad.

1 clove of garlic, peeled and grated

¼ -inch piece of ginger, peeled and grated

2 tablespoons chopped fresh coriander leaves

3 tablespoons lemon juice

2 tablespoons olive oil

Salt to taste

¼ teaspoon garam masala

½ lb. large sea scallops (about 9–10), washed and patted dry

1 tablespoon mustard oil *or* 1 tablespoon olive oil

1 hot green chili, finely chopped

½ teaspoon black mustard seeds

1 cup finely sliced green cabbage

½ red onion, finely sliced

Salt to taste

1 teaspoon white sesame seeds

½ teaspoon fennel seeds

1 small, green, unripened mango, peeled and cut into ½-inch cubes; scrape flesh attached to seed and reserve, discarding seed

In a bowl, combine the garlic, ginger, 1 tablespoon of fresh coriander leaves, 2 tablespoons of lemon juice, olive oil, salt, and garam masala. Toss in the scallops and marinate for at least 1 hour at room temperature, or overnight in the refrigerator. About 15 minutes before grilling, prepare the cabbage. If using the mustard oil, heat in a skillet on high until smoking. Immediately turn off the heat and add the green chili. (If you are using the olive oil, there is no need to heat to smoking point; just warm it over a high heat and proceed.) After a second, add the mustard seeds. When they begin to pop, add the cabbage and the red onion. Stir-fry for a minute, with the burner still off. Transfer the contents to a bowl and mix in the salt, the remaining 1 tablespoon of fresh coriander and 1 tablespoon of lemon juice. Cover and set aside. Toast the sesame seeds and the fennel seeds in a skillet over medium heat. As soon as they begin to darken (after a few seconds), remove from heat and set aside.

Put the scraped mango flesh into the cabbage salad, reserving the mango cubes for grilling. Thread the cubes onto skewers, and grill, covered, at medium-high heat for about 8 minutes or until lightly charred. If you have room, cook the scallops directly on the grill alongside the mango for about 5 minutes on each side, until lightly charred and cooked through. Halve the scallops, remove the mango from the skewers and add to the salad. Mix in the toasted sesame and fennel seeds, and toss well. Serve warm.

Shakarkandi ki Chaat

Sweet potatoes tossed with spices and lemon juice

Sweet potatoes are very popular in Uttar Pradesh and are used in many ways, *chaat* being one of the favorites. In villages, these potatoes are buried in the embers of the woodstove to cook slowly and acquire the aroma of wood smoke. They are then tossed with lemon juice and spices, and perhaps with some cooked peas and onions, and are eaten as a snack. They make a great salad, too, and can be prepared a day in advance.

2 medium sweet potatoes (about 1½ lb.)

Salt to taste

¼ teaspoon ground black pepper

½ teaspoon roasted ground cumin seeds

2–3 tablespoons lemon juice

SERVES 4

Put the potatoes in a microwave-safe bowl with enough water to cover, seal with plastic wrap, and microwave on high for 10 minutes. Drain and halve the potatoes lengthwise. Grill, covered, on medium heat until lightly charred and cooked through, about 15 to 20 minutes. Cool, peel, and wash, then dry with paper towels and cut into one-inch cubes. Add all the remaining ingredients and toss well. Serve chilled or at room temperature.

Jhinge aur simla mirch ka salat

Shrimp and roasted red pepper salad with sour cream, honey, and lime dressing

This flavorful salad with its sweet, sour, and creamy dressing is great for a light lunch when accompanied by soup and bread. Try teaming it with Cholam Soop (grilled corn and onion soup in a coconut and cream broth, page 23) or Bhune Tamatar ka Shorva (roasted tomato soup with cumin and fresh coriander, page 22).

2 cloves of garlic, peeled and grated

2 tablespoons vegetable oil

Salt to taste

1/4 teaspoon garam masala

1/2 teaspoon ground black pepper

1/2 lb. uncooked shrimp, fresh or frozen, peeled and deveined, washed and dried

1 medium sweet red pepper

2 tablespoons lemon juice

1/2 teaspoon roasted cumin

1 tablespoon honey

2 tablespoons sour cream

2 tablespoons chopped fresh coriander leaves

1 ripe tomato

2 cups shredded lettuce

SERVES 4

Mix the garlic with the oil, salt, garam masala, and black pepper. Toss in the shrimp and coat well with the marinade. Cover and set aside for 15 minutes. Roast the pepper in a covered barbecue at medium heat until charred, about 10 to 15 minutes. Set it aside in a paper bag to cool. Thread the shrimp onto skewers and grill on an open barbecue at medium heat until cooked and lightly charred, about 8 to 10 minutes. Peel the red pepper, wash off the charred skin, remove and discard the stem and seeds and cut into 1-inch pieces. Mix the lemon juice, cumin, honey, and sour cream together. Add salt and pepper to taste, then toss in the shrimp, red peppers, and chopped coriander leaves. Chop the tomato into chunks and add to the salad along with the shredded lettuce. Mix well and serve.

ṣalat-ɛ-kabob

Grilled ground meat kabobs tossed in a thickened yogurt, mint, and coriander dressing

If you have a few kabob pieces left after a barbecue, here is a good way to convert them into another meal. The yogurt dressing keeps the kabobs moist for days, and the salad tastes even better after extended marinating. If you have an assortment of ground meat kabobs, you could mix chicken and lamb, or even try a medley of chunky and ground meat kabobs. Any kabob recipe from this book would work well in this salad, and more vegetables, such as onions and green peppers, can be added. I like to serve Salat-e-Kabob wrapped up in warm flour tortillas or heaped over lettuce sandwiched in a roll.

4 tablespoons plain yogurt (not low-fat)

Salt to taste

¼ teaspoon black pepper

1 teaspoon lemon juice

½ teaspoon roasted ground cumin seeds

1 small hot green chili, finely chopped (optional)

¼ -inch piece of ginger, peeled and grated

1 clove of garlic, peeled and grated

1 tablespoon finely chopped fresh mint leaves

1 tablespoon finely chopped fresh coriander leaves

1 medium tomato, deseeded and diced into ½ -inch cubes

4 ground-meat (chicken or lamb) skewered kabobs (4 oz.)

SERVES 4

Place a paper coffee filter inside a sieve and set the sieve over a bowl. Put the yogurt into the filter and let it drain for 15 minutes. Discard the liquid. Scrape the thickened yogurt into a bowl and add in all the remaining ingredients except the kabobs. Mix well. Slide the kabobs off the skewers and dice them into ½-inch to 1-inch pieces. Add them to the yogurt dressing and toss gently to mix.

Raitas and Chutneys

Zucchini ka Raita *Grilled zucchini in lightly spiced yogurt* **baingan ka Raita** *Roasted eggplant with sautéed onion in yogurt* **bhune tamatar aur pyaz ka Raita** *Roasted tomatoes and onion in yogurt spiced with mint and roasted cumin seeds* **kaddoo ka Raita** *Grilled pumpkin in spiced yogurt* **alu ka Raita** *Roasted potatoes in spiced yogurt* **thayir pachadi** *Cucumber with grilled potatoes, onion, and tomatoes in yogurt* **hare tamatar ki Chatni** *Sweet-and-sour green tomato chutney with dates* **khatti meethi tamatar ki Chatni** *Sweet, sour, and spicy tomato chutney with ginger* **jhatpat tamatar wali Chatni** *Quick grilled tomato salsa* **hare aam ki Chatni** *Roasted green mango chutney with fresh herbs, chilies, and roasted garlic* **aam ki launji** *Roasted green mangoes in a spicy sweet-and-sour sauce* **mint yogurt dip with Roasted garlic** **Roasted Red Pepper and garlic yogurt dip**

*R*aitas (yogurt relishes) are an oasis of calm on an Indian dinner plate. No matter how fiery the rest of the food, you can always rely on raitas to soothe and refresh. Raitas are a versatile way to serve up vegetables and fruit in soothing, cooling yogurt. Just about anything can be added to raitas: okra, spinach, potatoes, tomatoes, cucumber, pineapple, bananas, and even dumplings made of lentils or chickpea flour. I am so fond of raitas that I will even eat them mixed with plain cooked rice.

The hallmark of a well-thought-out Indian meal is its intricate balance of flavors. In contrast to cooling raitas, chutneys add zest to the food. The word chutney is derived from the Hindi word *chatna*, which literally means to lick. Good chutney will leave you licking your fingers! The ingredients that go into the making of chutney range from herbs, vegetables, fresh fruits, dried fruits, and nuts. Chutneys can be sweet, sour, spicy, hot, or any combination of these.

Chutneys were perhaps the earliest examples of Indian food to reach Europe in the late seventeenth century. Preserving fruits and vegetables in sugar, vinegar, and spices kept them from spoiling during long sea voyages, and they provided a welcome break from the monotony of ship rations. Modified to suit European tastes, they became extremely popular, and recipes for Indian chutneys appeared in eighteenth-century English cookbooks. Descendants of these Anglo-Indian chutneys can still be found on grocery shelves.

In this chapter, you will find unusual ways to create raitas and chutneys with grilled ingredients. When grilling vegetables for raitas, leave them quite crisp and crunchy unless otherwise specified. Char them just enough to achieve that smoky flavor. You can use leftover raitas as salad dressings, or toss grilled meats in them to make a filling for wraps. Chutneys can also be used in many creative ways: as dips, as salad dressings, as sandwich spreads, as sauces, or as condiments. Let loose your imagination!

Zucchini ka Raita

Grilled zucchini in lightly spiced yogurt

Grilling the zucchini adds a wonderful, smoky flavor to the raita. Take care not to overcook the zucchini—its crispness contributes a welcome crunch. I like to season the raita with sautéed shallots and garlic when I am serving it at parties; however, that is not strictly necessary—it will taste just as good without it. This raita would go well with any chicken or lamb dish.

1 medium zucchini

1 teaspoon vegetable oil, for greasing

1 cup plain yogurt

¼ cup water

½ teaspoon roasted ground cumin seeds

Salt to taste

Optional seasonings:

1 small shallot, peeled and finely chopped

1 clove of garlic, peeled and finely chopped

1 tablespoon vegetable oil

¼ teaspoon cumin seeds

SERVES 4

Lightly grease the zucchini with the vegetable oil and grill on an open barbecue on medium-high heat until lightly charred but not limp, about 8 minutes. Cool, trim off the ends, and peel if desired. Finely chop the zucchini and set aside. Beat the yogurt with a spoon and add the water, roasted ground cumin seeds, and salt. Mix well, then add the zucchini.

If adding the optional seasonings, heat 1 tablespoon of vegetable oil in a skillet over a medium flame and add the cumin seeds. After a few seconds, add the shallot and garlic. Sauté for 2 to 3 minutes or until lightly browned. Cool and add to the raita. Mix well and serve.

baingan ka raïta

Roasted eggplant with sautéed onion in yogurt

Eggplant is an unusual vegetable to use in a raita, but I am so fond of both raitas and eggplant in any form that I find the combination irresistible. I am not alone; I happen to know people who substitute this raita for mayonnaise in their ham and cheese sandwiches! Baingan ka Raita could even double as a vegetarian side dish. The grilled eggplant adds a smoky flavor and a meaty texture to the yogurt. You could serve this raita with any chicken or lamb dish and with rice or naan.

1 small eggplant (½ lb.), washed

1 tablespoon vegetable oil

½ teaspoon cumin seeds

1 small onion, peeled and finely chopped

1 clove of garlic, peeled and finely chopped

¼ -inch piece of ginger, peeled and finely chopped

¼ teaspoon cayenne pepper

1 cup plain yogurt

¼ cup water

Salt to taste

½ teaspoon roasted ground cumin seeds

SERVES 4

Poke the eggplant in several places with a skewer or a sharp knife and grill, covered, on low heat for about 20 minutes. The eggplant should be completely softened and should smell roasted by the end of the cooking time. Cool it to room temperature, then cut off the stem and peel off the skin. On a chopping board, mash the pulp well with a fork. In a skillet, warm the oil over medium-high heat and add the cumin seeds. After a few seconds, add the chopped onion. Sauté for about 2 to 3 minutes until lightly browned, then add the garlic, ginger, and cayenne pepper. Remove the pan from the stove. With a spoon, beat the yogurt until it is smooth. Add the water, salt, and roasted cumin. Mix, then add the mashed eggplant and the onions from the pan. Stir well to mix, cover, and let the raita rest for ½ an hour for the flavors to mingle. This raita can also be prepared up to 2 days in advance if kept refrigerated.

bhune tamatar aur pyaz ka raita

Roasted tomatoes and onion in yogurt spiced with mint and roasted cumin seeds

If you want to fix up a quick raita for a side dish, this is a useful recipe to have on hand. The yogurt base can be readied ahead of time, and the vegetables don't take too long to grill. Take care to leave them quite crunchy as they come off the barbecue; char them just a little bit. You can also use leftover raita as a topping for kabob-stuffed pita pocket bread or as a spread for flat bread wraps before stuffing and rolling them up.

2 medium
tomatoes, halved

1 medium onion,
peeled and
halved

1 cup plain yogurt

½ cup water

Salt to taste

½ teaspoon roasted
ground cumin
seeds

¼ teaspoon ground
black pepper

½ teaspoon dried
powdered mint
leaves (optional)
or 1 tablespoon
finely chopped
fresh mint leaves

SERVES 4

Grill the vegetables, uncovered, on medium-high heat until lightly charred, about 5 to 8 minutes. Peel the tomatoes, if desired, and finely chop, reserving any accumulated juices. Finely chop the onion and set aside. With a spoon, beat the yogurt until smooth and add the water. Mix, then add all the remaining ingredients. Add the chopped vegetables as well as the reserved tomato juice and stir again, gently, to mix. Serve chilled or at room temperature.

kaddoo ka raita

Grilled pumpkin in spiced yogurt

Indian weddings are long, boisterous affairs that last 4 to 5 days. The numerous ceremonies are interspersed with many elaborate feasts, which are occasions for family, friends, and even casual acquaintances to gather. The food served at Hindu weddings is always vegetarian, and when pumpkins are in season this raita almost always forms a part of wedding festivities in Uttar Pradesh. It is often served with *puris* (deep fried wheat bread) and vegetables. Kaddoo ka Raita tastes better made a day in advance, and can also be served with any rice dish and with Tandoori Murgh Kari (chicken marinated in sautéed onions, tomatoes, and spices, page 68).

1 lb. peeled
  pumpkin

2½ cups water

1½ cups plain yogurt

Salt to taste

1 teaspoon roasted
  ground cumin
  seeds

SERVES 4

Scrape away and discard all the seeds and fiber clinging to the pumpkin and cut it into 1-inch pieces. Put the pieces in a microwave-safe bowl and cover with 1½ cups of water. Microwave on high for 8 minutes, then drain and cool. Skewer the pumpkin and grill, covered, on medium-high heat for about 10 minutes. The pumpkin should be soft and charred in spots when it is done. Slide the pieces off the skewers into a bowl and mash them with a fork until smooth. Beat the yogurt with a spoon until smooth. Mix in remaining 1 cup of water, salt, and roasted ground cumin seeds. Add the mashed pumpkin and stir well to mix. Serve the raita chilled or at room temperature.

alu ka raita

Roasted potatoes in spiced yogurt

I often roast potatoes at the end of a barbecue and put them away for later use. They come in handy when I run out of vegetables to put in my raitas. Sometimes I mash the potatoes coarsely with a fork, instead of slicing them, to add some texture to the yogurt base. You can serve this raita with any lamb dish of your choice.

2 medium potatoes

1 cup plain yogurt

½ cup water

½ teaspoon roasted ground cumin seeds

¼ teaspoon cayenne pepper

Salt to taste

1 tablespoon chopped fresh coriander leaves

SERVES 4

Put the potatoes in a microwave-safe bowl with enough water to cover, seal with plastic wrap, and cook on high for 8 minutes. Drain, wrap each potato in foil, and place on a grill, covered, on medium heat to finish cooking. Roast the potatoes for about 10 minutes or until they are tender. Remove them from the foil and allow to cool. Peel and finely chop them. Beat the yogurt with a spoon until smooth and add the water, all the spices, and the fresh coriander leaves. Mix again, then add the chopped potatoes. Stir gently and serve chilled or at room temperature.

thayir pachadi

Cucumber with grilled potatoes, onion, and tomatoes in yogurt

Raitas in southern India are frequently spiced with mustard seeds and curry leaves, with perhaps a finely chopped green chili for an added edge. Fresh curry leaves are readily available in most Indian grocery stores and can be kept refrigerated in a plastic bag for up to 2 weeks. They have a very unusual taste that intensifies when the leaves are fried in hot oil until crisp and then mixed into the dish. If you have trouble finding fresh curry leaves, you can substitute the same amount of dried curry leaves.

1 medium potato

1 medium onion, peeled

1 medium tomato, halved

1 medium cucumber

1½ cups plain yogurt

½ cup water

Salt to taste

1 tablespoon vegetable oil

½ teaspoon black mustard seeds

10 curry leaves

1 hot green chili, finely chopped

¼ teaspoon cayenne pepper

1 tablespoon chopped fresh coriander leaves

SERVES 4

Put the potato in a microwave-safe bowl with enough water to cover, seal with plastic wrap, and cook on high for 5 minutes. Drain and set aside. Roast all the vegetables except the cucumber, uncovered, on medium-high heat for about 7 to 10 minutes. Do not let them soften, just lightly char them. Cool and finely chop the onion and the tomato, peeling and deseeding the tomato if desired. Peel the potato and the cucumber and finely chop. Beat the yogurt with a spoon until smooth, then add the water and salt. Mix again, then put in all the chopped vegetables. Stir lightly. In a skillet, heat the oil over a medium flame and put in the mustard seeds. As soon as they begin to pop, add the curry leaves and green chili. Cook for 1 minute, then add the cayenne pepper. Remove from heat immediately and pour the spiced oil over the yogurt. Mix in the fresh coriander and serve.

hare Tamatar ki Chatni

Sweet-and-sour green tomato chutney with dates

When the first frost hits your vegetable garden and you are left with a lot of green tomatoes, try making some of this chutney. You can easily double the recipe and freeze extra batches for winter—the roasted aroma captured in the chutney is very welcome when snow is falling outside! This chutney tastes good in sandwiches and can also be used as a dip for grilled chicken and seafood dishes.

3 medium green
 tomatoes, halved

1 tablespoon
 vegetable oil

¼ teaspoon fennel
 seeds

¼ teaspoon cumin
 seeds

¼ teaspoon onion
 seeds (kalonji)

2 green cardamom

2 cloves

5 whole black
 peppercorns

¼ -inch stick
 cinnamon

¼ teaspoon
 turmeric

½ cup water

Salt to taste

¼ teaspoon cayenne
 pepper

2 tablespoons sugar

10 pitted dates,
 sliced in 3 pieces

1 tablespoon
 vinegar

SERVES 4 TO 6

Grill the tomatoes, covered, on medium heat until lightly charred, about 10 minutes, turning them over to cook evenly. Cool and peel, then chop each tomato half into three pieces. Set aside. In a skillet, heat the oil over a medium-high flame. Put in the fennel seeds, cumin seeds, onion seeds, cardamom, cloves, peppercorns, and cinnamon. As soon as the whole spices puff up and darken, add the turmeric. Stir quickly for a second, then pour in the water; stand back as you do so—it will splutter. Add the salt, cayenne, and sugar. Stir to mix, then gently add the chopped tomatoes. Bring to a boil, then reduce heat to low and simmer for about 5 to 8 minutes, or until the chutney has thickened a bit. Add the dates and the vinegar and turn off the heat. Let the pan sit on the stove as it cools to room temperature. The chutney will keep in the refrigerator for at least 10 days.

khattī meethī tamatar ki Chatni

Sweet, sour, and spicy tomato chutney with ginger

Tomato chutney to an Indian is a lot like ketchup to an American. It can accompany meals or serve as a dip for appetizers. As a child I would spread it on sandwiches for a quick after-school snack. When I was looking for a good tomato chutney recipe, I found that there were as many versions of it as there are cooks. So, I consulted my mother and mother-in-law, combined their two recipes, and here is the result. It can be kept frozen for as long as you want, and is a good way to use all those extra tomatoes from your garden.

4 medium red tomatoes (1 lb.)

2 tablespoons vegetable oil

2 whole cloves

2 whole cardamom

½ -inch stick cinnamon

8 whole black peppercorns

1 bay leaf

½ -inch piece of ginger, finely grated or minced

1 hot green chili, chopped, or ¼–½ teaspoon cayenne pepper

Salt to taste

3 tablespoons sugar

2 tablespoons vinegar

SERVES 4

Wrap each tomato in foil and grill, covered, on medium heat for about 20 minutes. They should be soft when they are done. Cool. Remove tomatoes from foil, saving all accumulated juices. Peel them and mash well with a fork, adding the reserved juices from the foil cups. (At this point, you may wish to strain the pulp through a sieve, though this is not normally done in Indian homes.) In a skillet, heat the oil over a medium flame and add all the whole spices and the bay leaf. As soon as they darken and puff up, add the ginger and green chili, if using them. Sauté for 1 minute and then mix in the tomato pulp. Bring to a boil, then reduce heat to medium low and stir in the salt as well as the cayenne, if using it. Cook, stirring frequently, for about 15 minutes. The chutney should be quite thick when it is done. Mix in the sugar and the vinegar and cook for 5 minutes more. Remove from heat and let cool.

You can serve this chutney at room temperature or cold. It will keep in the refrigerator for at least 2 weeks.

Jhatpat Tamatar wali Chatni

Quick grilled tomato salsa

The flavor of Mexican food always reminds me of Indian cooking. Many spices are common to the two cuisines, such as ground cumin seeds, fresh coriander, and chili peppers. In my family we often eat salsa in place of chutney, and over the years I evolved an Indianized version that combines the best of both recipes. You can serve it as a dip for barbecued meats, or you can toss chopped-up kabobs into it for a salad-like dish. Extra batches can be frozen for future use.

1 medium red
onion, peeled

2 cloves of garlic,
peeled

4 medium red ripe
tomatoes (about
1 lb.), halved

1 medium sweet
green pepper

Salt to taste

½ teaspoon roasted
ground cumin
seeds

½ teaspoon ground
black pepper

¼ teaspoon garam
masala

2 tablespoons
chopped fresh
coriander leaves

3 tablespoons
lemon juice

½ teaspoon Tabasco

SERVES 6

Grill the onion, garlic, tomatoes, and green pepper, uncovered, at medium-high heat until lightly charred, turning for evenness. The garlic will be the first to be done, about 5 to 7 minutes. The tomatoes should be next, about 10 minutes; then the onion, about 15 minutes; and lastly the pepper about 15 to 20 minutes, which should be nicely blackened all over by the time it is done. Put the pepper in a brown paper bag to cool. Meanwhile, quarter the onion, coarsely chop the garlic, and put them in a food processor or blender along with the tomatoes and all the remaining ingredients. Remove the pepper from the bag and peel off the charred skin. Wash under running water and dry with paper towels. Cut off the stem and seeds from the pepper, chop it coarsely, and add it to the food processor. Pulse it a few times until you have a chunky blend of salsa. If you want a smoother blend, pulse it a little longer. Transfer to a bowl and serve. This salsa should keep in the refrigerator for up to a week.

hare aam ki chatni

Roasted green mango chutney with fresh herbs, chilies,
and roasted garlic

A green herb chutney is a must at every Indian meal. The chutney is ground fresh daily and placed in the center of the table at dinnertime. It also serves as a dip for snacks such as deep-fried *pakoras* (dumplings) and *samosas* (deep-fried triangular pastry stuffed with spicy potatoes and peas). There are many variations of chutneys, some without any mint, others with tomatoes or yogurt. When in season, green unripe mangoes are usually added to the chutney to make it sour. Although the mango is not generally grilled before being added to the chutney, as I do here, grilling adds a unique aroma to the dish. It makes a great accompaniment for all kinds of barbecued foods, as a spread for sandwiches, or as a salad dressing. I have even successfully used it as a sauce for grilled food.

1 medium unripe green cooking mango, washed

2 cloves of garlic, peeled

1 hot green chili

½ -inch piece of ginger

1 cup loosely packed fresh mint leaves, washed and drained

1½ cups loosely packed fresh coriander leaves, washed and drained

Salt to taste

½ teaspoon roasted ground cumin seeds

¼ teaspoon cumin seeds

¼ cup water

SERVES 4

Grill the mango, covered, on low heat for about 30 minutes, or until the inside is slightly soft and the outside is well roasted. While the mango is roasting, wrap the cloves of garlic in foil and roast for about 7 to 10 minutes or until they are soft. Cool them both. Thoroughly scoop out all the pulp from the mango, discarding the skin and the seeds. Put the mango pulp and all the remaining ingredients in a blender and blend until smooth, adding an extra tablespoon of water if necessary. Transfer to a bowl and refrigerate. This chutney will keep for up to 2 weeks.

āam kĭ launjĭ

Roasted green mangoes in a spicy sweet-and-sour sauce

Mangoes excite a passion in Indians that is unfathomable to anyone who considers them to be just another fruit. Each region of the country has its own favored variety, the comparative merits of which are hotly debated by connoisseurs. Mangoes have even been the subjects of art, inspiring beautiful Paisley designs in paintings and fabrics. They have become a part of the cuisine and the basis of a number of dishes: mangoes that fall from the tree before ripening are used for pickles or made into chutneys; ripe mangoes are used in raitas, salads, and a myriad of other ways. This simple, delicious dish is very popular in the northern Indian state of Uttar Pradesh. When my mother makes this dish, she always puts the mango seed in the sauce along with the mango pieces. Cooked this way, the seed acquires all the sweet, sour, and spicy characteristics of the sauce and is great fun to suck on. You could serve it as a dipping sauce for appetizers. I even thin it with a little vinegar to use as a marinade for shrimp and as a sauce for grilled chicken.

1 medium unripe green cooking mango (about 1 lb.)

2 tablespoons vegetable oil

¼ teaspoon cumin seeds

¼ teaspoon onion seeds (kalonji)

½ teaspoon turmeric

¼ teaspoon cayenne pepper

¼ cup water

Salt to taste

1 teaspoon ground fennel seeds

1 tablespoon golden raisins

2 tablespoons sugar

½ teaspoon garam masala

SERVES 4

Roast the mango, covered, on a medium-hot barbecue for about 45 minutes or until tender. Cool and peel away the skin, scraping and reserving all the pulp and discarding the seed. In a skillet, heat the oil over a medium flame and add the cumin and onion seeds. As soon as they splutter, add the turmeric and cayenne. Immediately add the water, standing back as you do because it will spatter. Reduce heat to medium low and add the salt, fennel, and raisins. Cook for 3 to 4 minutes, then add the mango pulp. Stir well and cook for another 3 to 4 minutes. Add the sugar and garam masala and mix well. Keep unused portion refrigerated; it will last for at least 10 days.

mint yogurt dip with roasted garlic

Mint and yogurt are perhaps the most popular combination for a dip. Indian restaurants always place a bowl of this dip alongside their tandoori preparations: take a piece of naan, wrap it around a morsel of kabob, and dip it in the yogurt. Grilled, peeled, and chopped tomatoes can also be added to this dip for a change of taste.

2 cloves of garlic, peeled

½ cup plain yogurt

½ cup loosely packed fresh mint leaves, washed and drained

¼ cup water

Salt to taste

¼ teaspoon ground black pepper

SERVES 4

Wrap the garlic in foil and roast, covered, on medium heat until soft. This should take about 8 to 10 minutes. Mash the pulp with a fork or chop it finely. Beat the yogurt with a spoon until smooth. In a blender, blend the mint leaves and ¼ cup water to a fine paste. Add to the yogurt along with all the remaining ingredients and the garlic. Stir well to mix. Keep refrigerated until ready to serve.

Roasted Red Pepper and Garlic Yogurt Dip

Dips are not commonly served in most Indian homes. Traditionally, raitas and chutneys are used for a similar purpose—to soothe, refresh, and enliven the palate. However, I find that Indian ingredients make great dips that are ideal for serving with seafood and appetizers. I make my dips thicker than *raitas* and use whatever ingredients are available in the refrigerator. I always serve dip with barbecued Indian fish dishes for spreading or dunking. You can serve the following recipe chunky, as I describe it below, or lightly mince the red pepper and garlic in a food processor for a smoother dip.

1 medium sweet red pepper

1 clove of garlic, peeled

½ cup plain (low-fat) yogurt

¼ teaspoon roasted ground cumin seeds

Salt to taste

¼–½ teaspoon ground black pepper

2 tablespoons chopped fresh coriander leaves

SERVES 4

Roast the pepper and garlic in a covered grill on medium-high heat, turning them for even charring. The garlic should only take about 8 to 10 minutes to char, while the pepper should be done in about 15 minutes. Put the pepper in a paper bag to cool, then peel, wash, deseed, and chop finely into a bowl. Finely chop the garlic and add to the pepper. Beat the yogurt with a spoon until smooth and mix it into the red pepper and garlic. Add the remaining ingredients and stir to mix. Serve chilled or at room temperature.

Chicken

Calcutta Egg Rolls *Wraps stuffed with egg and chicken* **Murgh Kasoori**
Skewers of ground chicken marinated with fried onion and dried fenugreek leaves
Kaju Reshmi Seekh Kabobs *Ground-chicken kabobs minced with cashew
nuts and spices* **Kabob Tamatari** *Ground-chicken kabobs marinated with sun-
dried tomatoes, roasted peppers, and sautéed onions* **Murgh Tikka** *Chicken breast
marinated in thickened yogurt and spices* **Moghlai Tikka** *Chicken breast and
pineapple chunks marinated in almonds, cashew nuts, coconut, and cream* **Kashmiri
Murgh Elaichi** *Chicken breast marinated with yogurt, cardamom, and fennel*
Sindhi Elaichi Murgh *Chicken breast marinated in cardamom, black pepper,
yogurt, and fresh coriander* **Soya Murgh** *Morsels of chicken breast marinated in
soy sauce, vinegar, sesame oil, and spices* **Tandoori Murgh Kari** *Chicken marinated in sautéed onions, tomatoes, and spices* **Aadoo Murgh** *Chicken breast marinated with tomatoes and spices and grilled with fresh peaches* **bhuna Murga
Saagwala** *Chicken marinated with spinach, fresh coriander, and spices* **Tandoori**

Murgh *Chicken drumsticks marinated in yogurt, spices, and herbs* **hara Murga** *Chicken marinated in puréed green tomatoes and sour cream* **Murgh ka Soola** *Chicken marinated with sautéed onions* **Murgh kashmiru** *Chicken marinated in tamarind, ground fennel seeds, and ginger* **tandoori Murgh Vindaloo** *Chicken marinated with sautéed onions, vinegar, and spices* **Chili Chicken** *Chicken marinated in green chilies and tamarind* **bharvan Murgh** *Chicken thighs marinated in sour cream and spices and stuffed with sautéed onions, mushrooms, and bread crumbs*

Soon after our wedding, my husband and I holidayed in Kashmir. We stayed in Gulmarg, a small mountain resort, from which we had a spectacular view of the snow-capped Himalayan peaks. Our cabin, nestled among the pines, came with its own cook—Ghulam Nabi. The day we arrived he asked if we would like chicken for dinner and, being very fond of Kashmiri food, we of course said yes. He headed off down the mountain to the nearest village to get supplies. A while later we spotted him trudging back up the path carrying a loudly protesting chicken tucked under his arm. He disappeared behind the cabin and a few minutes later the squawks came to an abrupt end. That night the chicken curry looked delicious but I couldn't bring myself to try any. I felt that I had too intimate an acquaintance with it. Ever since then I've had mixed feelings when my grocer tells me the chicken is really fresh—to me there is such a thing as being *too* fresh!

Despite this experience, chicken remains my favorite barbecue food. (I sometimes think that if Ghulam Nabi had grilled the chicken that day, I might have been tempted to eat it!) Chicken is at its best when cooked tandoori style. Marinated in yogurt, herbs, and spices, it is a staple of Indian restaurant menus. Tandoori chicken was the first dish I tried cooking on my barbecue, and was so encouraged by my success that I went on to experiment with other kinds of marinades for chicken. When I invite friends who have never eaten tandoori food before, I include chicken in the menu, because it appeals to just about everybody.

You can grill chicken in many different ways: mold seekh kabobs out of spiced ground chicken; skewer cubes of boneless chicken with onions, tomatoes, and peppers; or grill chicken drumsticks and thighs. Chicken's mild flavor can be paired with any marinade, so you can combine different ingredients to create your own recipes.

Some of these recipes are very simple to put together; others involve some sauce preparation, which can be done ahead of time to give the flavors a chance to mingle (and the cook a chance to rest!). If you try your hand at making seekh kabobs out of ground chicken, be sure to chill it for at least half an hour; this makes the chicken easier to mold onto the skewers. If you find that this is too hard to do, then shape the ground chicken into hamburger-like patties. You can substitute chicken breast where the recipe calls for drumsticks and thighs; just adjust the cooking times accordingly. I have not used any oil or butter for basting the chicken in these recipes, since the leftover marinade makes an excellent low-fat alternative—but if you wish to finish grilling by basting the chicken with a little butter, then by all means do so. As always, the recipes can be easily doubled or halved to suit your requirements.

Calcutta Egg Rolls

Wraps stuffed with egg and chicken

The city of Calcutta was the capital of the British Empire in India for over a century. During this time it was a center for trade and a meeting place for people from many cultures. This history is reflected in its remarkable cuisine, which draws inspiration from its native Bengali people, its Moghul and British rulers, and the Chinese traders who settled there. These popular egg rolls are a specialty of Calcutta; they are sold from every street corner there, but I have never seen them anywhere else in India. They are said to have originated at Naizam's restaurant, a Calcutta landmark. The simplest way to make these egg rolls at home is with store-bought wonton wrappers. I suggested using Soya Murgh (chicken breast marinated in soy sauce, vinegar, sesame oil, and spices, page 66) or Chili Paneer (cottage cheese marinated in green chilies, ginger, garlic, coriander, and soy sauce, page 126) as a filling, but you could use any of your favorite recipes from this book. In a pinch, even chopped onions with a squeeze of lemon juice could be stuffed in these rolls. They are a great way to use leftovers and can be a meal by themselves.

4 eggs

Salt to taste

Vegetable oil for shallow frying

8 store-bought wonton wrappers (about 5" X 5" in size)

1 recipe of Soya Murgh or Chili Paneer

SERVES 4

Break the eggs in a bowl and beat well with a fork. Add the salt and mix again. Warm a small skillet over medium heat and add a teaspoon of oil. Pour in about 3 tablespoons of the egg and spread it around to approximately the size of the wonton wrapper. Now place one wonton wrapper over the egg and scrape in all the egg seeping outside of it. When the underside of the egg is done to a light brown, flip it over and cook until the wonton side is lightly browned. Put the filling in a line in the center of the side with the egg and roll up the edges tightly around it. Slide it onto a plate and serve with chili sauce or chutney. Proceed similarly with the remaining wonton wrappers and eggs.

murgh kasoori

*Skewers of ground chicken marinated with fried onion
and dried fenugreek leaves*

My kids, who usually have to be coaxed into trying anything new,
instantly liked these kabobs. They call them "meat on a stick" and insist on having them every time I cook an Indian barbecued meal. They can be served with
a cucumber salad and naan. For a fancier dish you can serve the kabobs in
Tamatar Methi ka Masala (tomato fenugreek cream sauce, page 168) and have
rice on the side. They also make excellent appetizers, halved and served on a bed
of lettuce and sliced tomatoes.

2 tablespoons
vegetable oil

1 teaspoon cumin
seeds

1 medium onion,
peeled and
coarsely chopped

1 -inch piece of
ginger, peeled
and coarsely
chopped

2 cloves of garlic,
peeled and
coarsely chopped

1 large egg

½ teaspoon garam
masala

½ teaspoon ground
coriander seeds

½ teaspoon ground
cumin seeds

Salt to taste

¼–½ teaspoon ground
black pepper

¼ cup loosely
packed dried
fenugreek leaves

¼ cup fresh
coriander leaves
and tender
stems, washed
and drained well

1 lb. lean ground
chicken

Lemon juice

SERVES 4

In a skillet, warm the oil over medium
heat and add the cumin seeds. After a
few seconds add the chopped onion,
ginger, and garlic. Sauté for 5 minutes, or until the edges are lightly
browned. Cool and lift the pieces
from the oil with a slotted spoon,
leaving as much oil behind as possible. Pat the sautéed onion mixture
with a paper towel to get rid of the
excess oil. Mince the onions in a food
processor or blender. Scrape down

the sides of the bowl and add the egg, all the spices, the fenugreek leaves, and
the fresh coriander. Whirl once, then add the chicken. Blend for a few minutes
until everything is well mixed. Transfer to a bowl, cover, and refrigerate for at
least 1 hour. When ready to make kabobs, wet your hands lightly, shake off the
excess moisture, and make lemon-sized balls of the chicken mixture. Mold it

onto skewers in 4- to 6-inch-long sausage shapes, pressing the meat gently with your fingers to shape it. Grill, covered, in a medium-hot barbecue until lightly browned and cooked through, turning occasionally to ensure even cooking. This should take about 10 minutes. Uncover the grill, turn up the heat slightly, and char the kabobs for 2 minutes more. Slide the kabobs off the skewers and serve with a dash of lemon juice.

kaju reshmi seekh kabobs

Ground-chicken kabobs minced with cashew nuts and spices

Reshmi means silky, which aptly describes the smooth texture of these kabobs. The powdered cashew nuts, which are blended with the meat, contribute to the kabobs' soft melt-in-the-mouth quality. This is a rich dish and is usually reserved for banquets and special occasions. These kabobs also make great appetizers, halved and served with a chutney or dip.

1 medium onion, peeled and coarsely chopped

2 cloves of garlic, peeled and coarsely chopped

½ -inch piece of ginger, peeled and coarsely chopped

½ cup cashew nuts (unroasted and unsalted), powdered

Salt to taste

¼–½ teaspoon ground black pepper

½ teaspoon ground coriander seeds

½ teaspoon ground cumin seeds

½ teaspoon garam masala

1 large egg

1 lb. lean ground chicken

Lemon juice

SERVES 4

In a food processor, combine the onion, garlic, and ginger, and mince. Add the cashew nuts along with all the other spices and egg, and whirl to mix; then add the ground chicken and blend again. Transfer the mixture to a bowl, cover, and refrigerate for at least 1 hour.

When ready to grill, wet your hands lightly, shake off the excess moisture, and make lemon-sized balls of the chicken mixture. Mold them onto the skewers in 4- to 6-inch-long sausage shapes, pressing the meat gently with your fingers to make it stick. Grill, covered, on medium heat, turning occasionally for about 10 minutes. When the kabobs are cooked through and lightly browned, uncover the grill. Now turn up the heat slightly and char the kabobs for 2 minutes more. Slide them off the skewers, heap onto plates, and serve with a dash of lemon juice.

kabob tamatari

Ground-chicken kabobs marinated with sun-dried tomatoes, roasted peppers, and sautéed onions

If you associate sun-dried tomatoes with pastas and salads, try using them in Indian cooking to see how versatile they really are. I have successfully used them ground into chutneys, folded into herb butters, stuffed into Indian breads, and as marinades. In this recipe, they are ground with the meat and shaped into sausage-like rolls on skewers.

My friends Nina and Peter taught me the following method of making sun-dried tomatoes at home in the oven. Cut washed Italian plum tomatoes in half. Preheat the oven to 250°F. Put the tomatoes, cut side up, on an ungreased baking sheet and bake for 8 hours—no turning is necessary. Toward the end of cooking time, check occasionally to see if any of the tomatoes are done and remove the ones that are starting to burn. When the tomatoes are done, cool them and put them in freezer bags. You can freeze them indefinitely, and most of the time you don't need to thaw them before use—only if you're grinding with meat for kabobs.

2 tablespoons vegetable oil

1 teaspoon fennel seeds

½ teaspoon whole black pepper

2 medium onions, peeled and coarsely chopped

4 cloves of garlic, peeled and coarsely chopped

1 -inch piece of ginger, peeled and coarsely chopped

1 hot green chili, peeled and coarsely chopped

14 sun-dried tomato halves, drained if packed in oil or thawed if frozen

1 roasted sweet red pepper, peeled and deseeded

1 roasted sweet green pepper, peeled and deseeded

1 large egg

1 lb. lean ground chicken

2 tablespoons chickpea flour (besan) *or* all-purpose white flour

½ teaspoon garam masala

Salt to taste

Lemon juice

In a skillet, heat the oil over a medium-high flame and add the fennel seeds and black pepper. After a few seconds, add the chopped onions, garlic, ginger, and chili. Sauté until lightly browned, about 5 to 7 minutes. Remove from the oil with a slotted spoon and pat dry with a paper towel. Put the sautéed mixture in the container of a food processor. Add all the remaining ingredients except the lemon juice to the bowl. Process until everything is well blended. Transfer the contents to a mixing bowl and refrigerate for about 1 hour.

When ready to make kabobs, wet your hands lightly, shake off the excess water, and make lemon-sized balls of the chicken mixture. Now mold them onto skewers in 4- to 6-inch-long sausage shapes, pressing the meat gently in with your fingers to make it stick. Grill, covered, on medium heat until lightly browned and cooked through, turning occasionally to ensure even cooking. This should take about 10 minutes. Uncover the grill, turn up the heat slightly, and char the kabobs for 2 minutes more. Slide them off the skewers and serve with a dash of lemon juice.

Murgh Tikka

Chicken breast marinated in thickened yogurt and spices

Tikkas are pieces of boned chicken meat that have been marinated in spices and grilled. There are many varieties of tikkas; the spices and ingredients of the marinade vary according to the tastes and expertise of the cook. The recipe given here is for classic Murgh Tikka, which is Moghlai in origin. They make excellent appetizers when served with a dip, or they can be served in Makhani Tamatar ka Masala (tomato sauce with butter and cream, page 167) for an elegant entrée.

3 tablespoons plain yogurt, not low-fat

½ -inch piece of ginger, grated

2 cloves of garlic, grated

Salt to taste

½ teaspoon garam masala

½ teaspoon ground coriander seeds

½ teaspoon ground cumin seeds

½ teaspoon ground black pepper

1 tablespoon dried fenugreek leaves

1 tablespoon ketchup (optional)

½ lb. boneless, skinless chicken breast, cut into 1-inch cubes, washed, and dried

Lemon juice

SERVES 2

Place a coffee filter in a sieve set over a bowl and put the yogurt into it. Let it drain for 15 minutes. Scrape the thickened yogurt out of the filter and into a mixing bowl. Add the ginger and garlic to the yogurt, along with all the remaining ingredients except the lemon juice. Mix well, then toss in the chicken pieces. Coat them with the marinade, then cover and refrigerate for at least 4 hours, or overnight. When ready to grill, thread the chicken cubes onto skewers, about 5 to 6 per skewer, leaving a little gap between the pieces. Grill, covered, over medium heat. Turn occasionally and baste with any leftover marinade. When the tikkas are cooked through and lightly browned (about 10 to 12 minutes), uncover the grill and turn up the heat slightly. Char the chicken for 2 minutes more, then remove them from the skewers and heap onto a platter. Sprinkle liberally with lemon juice and serve hot.

moghlai tikka

Chicken breast and pineapple chunks marinated in almonds, cashew nuts, coconut, and cream

The Moghuls who came to India from Central Asia in the sixteenth century brought with them a heritage that blended Arab, Turkish, and Persian cultures. Hindu artists and craftsmen assimilated these influences and produced a unique culture that led to a remarkable flowering of art and architecture, of which the best-known example is the Taj Mahal. The Moghuls' love of rich living, displayed in the elegance of their courts, is also evident in the cuisine they bequeathed to India. Moghlai food is characterized by its lavish use of cream, nuts, and spices. In this recipe, the grilled pineapple adds a nice sweet-and-sour touch to the tikkas. Serve them with Badaami Seekh Kabobs (ground lamb marinated with fried onions and almonds, page 87) and naan.

½ -inch piece of ginger, grated or minced

¼ cup unroasted, unsalted almonds, finely powdered

¼ cup unroasted, unsalted cashew nuts, finely powdered

3 tablespoons fresh grated coconut

½ cup heavy cream

Salt to taste

½ teaspoon ground

black pepper

½ teaspoon garam masala

1 teaspoon ground fennel seeds

½ lb. boneless, skinless chicken breast, cut into 1-inch cubes, washed and dried

14 -oz. can of pineapple slices, drained and cut into 2-inch chunks

Lemon juice

SERVES 4

In a mixing bowl, combine all ingredients except the chicken, pineapple, and lemon juice. Mix well, then toss in the chicken and coat thoroughly with the marinade. Cover and refrigerate for at least 1 hour. When ready to cook, thread the chicken onto skewers, alternating with the pineapple chunks. Grill, covered, on medium heat, basting occasionally with the leftover marinade until lightly browned and cooked through, about 10 to 12 minutes. Uncover the barbecue, turn up the heat slightly, and char the chicken for 2 minutes more. Slide the chicken and pineapple off the skewers and heap onto a platter. Sprinkle liberally with lemon juice and serve.

kashmiri murgh Elaichi

Chicken breast marinated with yogurt, cardamom, and fennel

The spices you taste in an Indian dish are a tip-off to its region of origin. Kashmiri cooking can be identified by its extensive use of fennel seeds, cardamom, and dried ginger. The bright red hue of the dishes comes from Kashmiri chili peppers, which are mild in taste but add glorious color. Good-quality paprika would be an adequate substitute.

Because there is no garam masala added to this recipe (unusual in itself!), you will find that this chicken tastes different from other tandoori fare. It can be rolled up in a soft flour tortilla and served topped with Zucchini ka Raita (grilled zucchini in lightly spiced yogurt, page 38) and shredded lettuce.

½ -inch piece of ginger, grated or minced

2 cloves of garlic, grated or minced

Salt to taste

¼–½ teaspoon ground black pepper

¼–½ teaspoon paprika

½ teaspoon whole cumin seeds, finely powdered

2 teaspoons whole fennel seeds, finely powdered

15 whole green cardamom, finely powdered

1 cup plain yogurt (not low-fat)

2 lb. boneless, skinless chicken breast, cut into 1-inch cubes, washed and dried

Lemon juice

SERVES 4 TO 6

Combine the grated ginger, garlic, salt, pepper, paprika, powdered spices, and yogurt and mix well. Add the chicken and toss to coat well with the marinade. Cover and marinate in the refrigerator for 3 to 4 hours or longer. When ready to grill, lift the chicken pieces out of the marinade and thread onto skewers, about 5 to 6 on each. Leave a little gap between the pieces to ensure even cooking. Grill, covered, on medium heat until cooked through and lightly browned, about 10 to 12 minutes. Uncover the grill, turn up the heat slightly, and char the chicken for 2 minutes more. Slide the chicken pieces off the skewers and onto a plate. Serve sprinkled liberally with lemon juice.

sindhi elaichi murgh

Chicken breast marinated in cardamom, black pepper, yogurt, and fresh coriander

Alexander the Great and his army marched east from Greece on their journey of conquest, arriving in 323 BC on the banks of the Sindhu River, which flows through the province of Sindh. The Greeks called the river Indus, the name it still bears in English, and the country lying beyond the river became known as India. Ironically, the province of Sindh that gave its name to the whole country is no longer part of India: it lies in Pakistan. However, Sindhi migrants have carried their cuisine to all corners of India, where it is very popular. Sindhi food can be recognized by its abundant use of fresh coriander and cardamom.

4 tablespoons plain yogurt (not low-fat)

20 green cardamom, finely powdered

1 teaspoon whole black pepper, finely powdered

Salt to taste

½ teaspoon ground coriander seeds

1 cup packed fresh coriander leaves and tender upper stems, washed and drained well

1 green chili, deseeded if desired

½ cup diced tomatoes (fresh or canned)

1 lb. boneless, skinless chicken breast, cut into 1-inch pieces, washed and drained

Lemon juice

SERVES 4

Beat the yogurt with a spoon for a few minutes until it is smooth; add the ground cardamom and black pepper. Mix in the salt and ground coriander seeds. In a blender or food processor, combine the fresh coriander, green chili, and diced tomatoes. Whirl to a smooth purée. Add the purée to the yogurt mixture and mix well with a spoon. Now toss in the chicken pieces and coat well with the marinade. Cover and refrigerate for at least 4 hours or, preferably, overnight. When you are ready to grill, lift the pieces of chicken out of the marinade and thread onto skewers. Spread any remaining marinade on top of the skewered chicken. Grill the skewers, covered, over medium heat and cook until lightly browned on all sides. Flip the skewers now and then to ensure even cooking.

When all the skewers are done, which should take about 10 to 12 minutes, uncover the barbecue and turn up the heat slightly. Char the chicken for 2 minutes, then slide it off the skewers and heap onto a platter. Sprinkle lemon juice all over them and serve.

soya murgh

Chicken breast marinated in soy sauce, vinegar, sesame oil, and spices

I find the Hindu theory of reincarnation very attractive because I like the idea of being reborn in China—the better to indulge my passion for Chinese cuisine. I love Chinese food and quite often cook it at home. I find that Chinese ingredients such as soy sauce and sesame oil blend amazingly well with Indian ingredients like garam masala. And both cuisines use fresh coriander leaves, ginger, and garlic. In Soya Murgh, I combine all these flavors to create something that, while not traditional, is certainly delicious. For variety, you can intersperse the chicken with cubed onions and green peppers.

2 cloves of garlic, peeled

½ -inch piece of ginger

1 hot green chili (optional)

½ cup packed fresh coriander leaves, washed and well drained

3 tablespoons dark soy sauce

3 tablespoons white or rice vinegar

1 tablespoon sesame oil

½ teaspoon ground black pepper

½ teaspoon garam masala

1 teaspoon sugar

½ lb. boneless, skinless chicken breast, cut into 1-inch cubes, washed and drained

SERVES 2

In a food processor or blender, mince the garlic, ginger, chili, and fresh coriander leaves. Add all the remaining ingredients and blend until fairly smooth. Transfer contents to a mixing bowl and toss in the chicken pieces. Coat well with the marinade, cover, and refrigerate for 1 hour. When ready to grill, thread the pieces of chicken onto skewers and spread any remaining marinade over them. Grill, covered, at medium heat for about 10 minutes, or until the pieces are done to your liking. Turn the skewers once or twice for even cooking. Uncover the lid, turn up the heat slightly and char the chicken for 2 minutes more. To serve, slide chicken off the skewers and heap onto a plate.

Tandoori Murgh Kari

Chicken marinated in sautéed onions, tomatoes,
and spices

The word "curry," synonymous to the Western mind with all Indian food, does not exist in any Indian language. It could have originated from the Tamil word *kari* that refers to meat cooked in a spicy sauce. The all-purpose curry powder, so popular in the West, is not used in India. A special blend of spices known as *masala* is used for every dish, some of it ground fresh every day. An Indian cook would treat curry powder with the same disdain that an Italian chef reserves for canned pasta sauce. In this grilled version of the popular chicken curry, the chicken is first marinated in the traditional masala—a paste of onions, ginger, garlic, spices, and tomatoes—and then tossed back into the masala paste after being grilled, creating a bouquet of sautéed and grilled aromas. This dish can be served with naan and Kaju Methi Paneer ke Tikke (cottage cheese and green peppers in a sauce of cashew nuts, fenugreek leaves, tomatoes, and cream, page 128).

6 cloves of garlic, peeled and coarsely chopped

1 -inch piece of ginger, peeled and coarsely chopped

3 medium onions, peeled and coarsely chopped

4 tablespoons vegetable oil

1 teaspoon cumin seeds

1½ cups diced tomatoes (fresh or canned)

1 teaspoon turmeric

1 teaspoon garam masala

1 teaspoon ground coriander seeds

1 teaspoon ground cumin seeds

Salt to taste

¼–½ teaspoon cayenne pepper

2 lb. chicken thighs and/or drumsticks, skinned, washed, and dried

Lemon juice

SERVES 4

In a food processor, mince the garlic, ginger, and onion. In a skillet, heat the oil over a medium flame and add the cumin seeds. After a few seconds, add the minced onion mixture from the food processor. Sauté until lightly browned, about 8 to 10 minutes, stirring occasionally to prevent burning. Meanwhile, whirl the diced tomatoes in the food processor for 1 minute. When the onions are done, add the tomatoes and all the spices. Stir to mix and cook for another 5 minutes until slightly thickened. Transfer to a mixing bowl and allow to cool for a few minutes. Divide the marinade in half and set one half aside. With a sharp knife, make a few deep gashes in each chicken piece and add to the remaining marinade, thoroughly coating the pieces. Cover and refrigerate for at least 4 hours or, preferably, overnight. When ready to cook, lift out the pieces from the marinade and grill, covered, on medium-low heat. Turn occasionally until lightly browned and cooked through, about 20 to 25 minutes. Uncover the grill, turn up the heat slightly, and char the chicken lightly for a few minutes. When all the pieces are done, toss them in the reserved, warmed-up marinade and serve with a dash of lemon juice.

aadoo murgh

Chicken breast marinated with tomatoes and spices and grilled with fresh peaches

I got the idea of grilling chicken with fresh peaches after eating a popular Parsi dish in which chicken is cooked with dried apricots. Fresh peaches add a sweet and tangy flavor to the dish, and they grill well on the barbecue. When I make Aadoo Murgh for my family, I find that the grilled peaches get gobbled up first, with my kids insisting that next time I just make skewers of grilled peaches and forget about the chicken!

½ -inch piece of ginger

2 cloves of garlic, peeled

2 medium plum tomatoes

4 tablespoons lemon juice

2 tablespoons vegetable oil

Salt to taste

¼–½ teaspoon cayenne pepper

¼ teaspoon ground cumin seeds

¼ teaspoon ground coriander seeds

¼ teaspoon garam masala

½ lb. boneless, skinless chicken breast, cut into 1-inch pieces, washed and dried

2 medium peaches, peeled and pitted, cut into 1-inch pieces immediately prior to grilling

SERVES 2

In a food processor or blender, purée the ginger, garlic, and tomatoes. Add the lemon juice, vegetable oil, salt, cayenne, ground cumin, coriander, and garam masala. Whirl again to mix. Transfer the contents to a mixing bowl and toss in the chicken pieces. Coat well with the marinade, cover, and refrigerate for at least two hours. Lift the chicken out of its marinade and thread onto skewers, alternating with the peaches. Grill, covered, on medium-high heat for about 10 minutes. Flip the skewers occasionally and baste with the leftover marinade. If the peaches begin to burn before the chicken is done, you can remove them from the skewers and put the chicken directly on the grill to finish cooking. To serve, slide the chicken and peaches off the skewers and toss gently to mix.

bhuna murga saagwala

Chicken marinated with spinach, fresh coriander, and spices

If my son Varun were told that his favorite barbecued chicken dish had spinach in it, a vegetable he normally won't touch, he would be horrified. This is a well-kept secret at our house—he's actually eating spinach without even realizing it! Naan and tomato chutney are a wonderful complement.

½ lb. trimmed fresh spinach leaves, washed well

1 -inch piece of ginger, peeled

4 cloves of garlic, peeled

2 cups packed fresh coriander leaves and tender upper stems, washed well and drained

Salt to taste

¼–½ teaspoon ground black pepper

1 teaspoon garam masala

1 teaspoon ground coriander seeds

¾ teaspoon ground cumin seeds

1 cup plain yogurt (not low-fat)

2 lb. chicken pieces, drumsticks and/or thighs, skinned, washed, and dried

Lemon juice

SERVES 4

Put the spinach in a microwave-safe dish (do not add water). Cover with plastic wrap and microwave on high for 5 minutes. Lift the spinach out of the liquid and set in a colander or sieve to drain; discarding all accumulated liquid. In a food processor, mince the ginger and garlic. Add the spinach and fresh coriander and mince again. Add all the spices and the yogurt and whirl again to mix. Transfer the contents to a bowl. With a sharp knife, make a few deep gashes in each piece of chicken and evenly coat with the marinade. Cover and refrigerate for at least 4 hours. When ready to barbecue, lift the chicken out of its marinade and grill, covered, on medium-low heat, basting occasionally with the leftover marinade and turning the pieces for even cooking. When the chicken is cooked through and lightly browned (about 20 to 25 minutes), uncover, turn up the heat slightly and char lightly for a few minutes more. Serve with a sprinkling of lemon juice.

Tandoori Murgh

Chicken drumsticks marinated in yogurt, spices, and herbs

If you have ever eaten tandoori food, chances are that you have already tasted Tandoori Murgh. This is the best-known and most popular dish of tandoori cuisine and features prominently in Indian restaurant menus. The traditional recipe uses saffron, which infuses the chicken with a rich aroma and gives it a warm red hue. Because saffron is too expensive for most restaurants, they resort to using food coloring, which turns the chicken an alarming orange but does nothing for its taste. In this recipe, the chicken gets its color from paprika. The color might not be as bright as you see in restaurants, but the flavor should be every bit as good.

1 cup plain yogurt (not low-fat)

4 cloves of garlic, peeled and grated

1 -inch piece of ginger, peeled and grated

Salt to taste

¾ teaspoon garam masala

¾ teaspoon ground coriander seeds

½ teaspoon ground cumin seeds

1 tablespoon dried fenugreek leaves

¼–½ teaspoon ground black pepper

¼–½ teaspoon Hungarian paprika

½ teaspoon roasted ground cumin seeds

½ teaspoon whole cumin seeds

1 tablespoon finely chopped fresh coriander leaves

2 lb. chicken drumsticks, skinned, washed, and dried

Lemon juice

SERVES 4

Beat the yogurt with a spoon to break up the lumps, then mix in the grated garlic and ginger. Now add all the remaining ingredients except the lemon juice and mix well. With a sharp knife, make deep gashes in each piece of chicken and toss the pieces into the marinade to coat. Cover and refrigerate overnight or for at least 4 hours. When ready to grill, lift the chicken out of the marinade and grill, covered, on medium-low heat for about 20 to 25 minutes. Turn the pieces occasionally while they are cooking and baste with the leftover marinade. When they are cooked through and lightly browned, uncover the barbecue and turn up the heat slightly. Now char the chicken lightly for a few minutes more. Heap the pieces on a platter and sprinkle liberally with lemon juice. Serve hot.

haRa muRga

Chicken marinated in puréed green tomatoes and sour cream

Green tomatoes and sour cream are used abundantly in the marinade of Hara Murga, lending a pleasant tartness to the taste. This recipe is very quick and easy to put together and tastes better if you let the chicken marinate overnight in the refrigerator. Serve it with a raita (yogurt relish) or tomato chutney.

4 cloves of garlic, peeled and chopped

1 -inch piece of ginger, peeled and chopped

1 small onion, peeled and chopped

2 medium green tomatoes (about ¾ lb.)

1 hot green chili

3 tablespoons sour cream

Salt to taste

¼–½ teaspoon ground black pepper

1 teaspoon garam masala

1 teaspoon ground coriander seeds

1 teaspoon ground cumin seeds

1 teaspoon sugar

2 lb. chicken pieces, drumsticks and/or thighs, skinned, washed, and dried

Lemon juice

SERVES 4

Put all the ingredients except the lemon juice in a blender and purée to a smooth paste; transfer the contents to a mixing bowl. With a sharp knife, make a few deep gashes in each chicken piece and add to the bowl. Mix well to coat with the marinade, cover, and refrigerate for at least 4 hours or, preferably, overnight. When ready to grill, lift the chicken out of the marinade and grill, covered, on medium-low heat for about 20 to 25 minutes. Turn occasionally and baste with the leftover marinade when needed. Uncover the barbecue, increase heat to medium high, and grill chicken a few minutes more, or until lightly charred. Serve with a dash of lemon juice.

murgh ka soola

Chicken marinated with sautéed onions

Rajasthan, a state in western India, was forged from the kingdoms of the Rajputs. This land, with its fairytale fortresses, turbaned warriors, and camels swaying across the desert dunes, is perhaps the closest that India gets to romantic Western images of the country. Rajput clans fought epic battles against Moghul invaders in the sixteenth century, but were defeated and later became their close allies. Rajasthani food has been molded by the hunting traditions of the Rajput warriors and by the tastes of their Moghul rulers. Murgh ka Soola was traditionally cooked at the end of a hunting party when meats were skewered and grilled over an open fire. The dish employs a marinade rich with the flavor of sautéed onions, which impart a smoky sweetness to the chicken.

2 tablespoons vegetable oil

½ teaspoon cumin seeds

2 large onions, peeled and coarsely chopped

1 -inch piece of ginger, peeled and coarsely chopped

4 cloves of garlic, peeled and coarsely chopped

1 cup plain yogurt (not low-fat)

Salt to taste

¼–½ teaspoon ground black pepper

1 teaspoon ground coriander seeds

¾ teaspoon ground cumin seeds

1 teaspoon garam masala

2 lb. chicken drumsticks and/or thighs, skinned, washed, and dried

Lemon juice

Fresh coriander leaves for garnish

SERVES 4

In a skillet, heat the oil over a medium-high flame and put in the cumin seeds. After a few seconds, add the chopped onions, ginger, and garlic. Sauté for 4 to 5 minutes, or until the edges of the onion are lightly browned. Remove from heat and transfer the onion mixture, oil and all, to a blender. Blend to a paste, scraping down the sides of the jar once. Add the yogurt and all the other spices and blend once again, then transfer to a large bowl. With a sharp knife, make a few deep gashes on each piece of chicken and add to the bowl. Rub the marinade in, cover, and refrigerate for 4 hours or longer. Lift the chicken out of its marinade and grill, covered, on medium-low heat. Baste occasionally with the leftover marinade, turning the pieces to ensure even cooking. When the chicken has cooked through (about 20 to 25 minutes), uncover, turn up the heat slightly and lightly char for a few minutes. Serve sprinkled with lemon juice and garnished with fresh coriander leaves.

murgh kashmiri

Chicken marinated in tamarind, ground fennel seeds, and ginger

In Kashmir, eggplant is often cooked in a tamarind and fennel sauce. I like the dish so much that I decided to experiment with the basic recipe, substituting chicken for the eggplant and grilling it on the barbecue. The result is a pleasant sweet-and-sour charbroiled taste rich with the aroma of tamarind and fennel seeds.

A lime-sized piece of seedless tamarind (4 oz.), soaked in ½ cup hot water for at least 1 hour (it should soften and absorb most of the water), *or*

2 tablespoons tamarind paste, dissolved in 4 tablespoons hot water

1 -inch piece of ginger, grated

¼ cup vegetable oil

Salt to taste

¼–½ teaspoon ground black pepper

½ teaspoon ground coriander seeds

½ teaspoon ground cumin seeds

½ teaspoon garam masala

2 teaspoons fennel seeds, powdered

1 teaspoon sugar

2 lb. chicken pieces, drumsticks and/or thighs, skinned, washed, and dried

SERVES 4

Mash the tamarind with a fork and squeeze through a fine sieve set over a bowl, extracting all the pulp and discarding the fibers and seeds. (You may omit this step if using the tamarind paste.) Add the ginger to the tamarind pulp; then add the oil and the remaining ingredients, mixing well. With a sharp knife, make a few deep gashes on each piece of chicken and rub the tamarind paste into the chicken pieces. Cover and refrigerate for at least 4 hours or, preferably, overnight. When ready to grill, cover the chicken and cook on medium-low heat until tender, turning occasionally. This should take about 20 to 25 minutes. Uncover the lid, turn up the heat slightly, and char for a few minutes more.

Tandoori Murgh Vindaloo

Chicken marinated with sautéed onions, vinegar, and spices

Goa, located on India's west coast, became a Portuguese colony soon after Vasco da Gama, who found the first sea route from Europe to India, arrived in 1498. It remained under Portuguese rule, and a center of the spice trade, until 1962, when it reverted to India. Five centuries of Portuguese influence have left an indelible impression on the culture, religion, and cuisine of Goa. Even today, the Latin influences are evident in the cathedrals, the carnival celebrations, and the cantinas that are found all over Goa. The food reflects the same medley of Portuguese and Indian flavors. The word *vindaloo*, which means a dish cooked in vinegar and garlic, has Portuguese origins. Vindaloo is almost always made with pork; however, I find that the basic recipe can be adapted to any kind of meat or poultry. The traditional version uses a lot of chilies, though that is a matter of taste and can be adjusted accordingly. You may serve it with Bhune Alu Masaledaar (crispy potatoes marinated in spices, page 132), raita (yogurt relish), and naan.

3 tablespoons
vegetable oil

½ teaspoon black
mustard seeds

3 medium onions,
peeled and
coarsely chopped

6 cloves of garlic,
peeled and
coarsely chopped

1 -inch piece of
ginger, peeled
and coarsely
chopped

2 hot green chilies,
chopped

½ cup distilled
white vinegar

Salt to taste

½ teaspoon ground
black pepper

1 teaspoon
turmeric

1 teaspoon garam
masala

1 teaspoon ground
coriander seeds

1 teaspoon ground
cumin seeds

2 lb. chicken
drumsticks
and/or thighs,
skinned, washed,
and dried

In a skillet, heat the oil over medium-high heat and add the mustard seeds. After a few seconds, add the chopped onions, garlic, ginger, and green chilies. Sauté for 5 minutes, or until they are lightly browned. Add all the spices and sauté for 1 minute. Remove from heat and cool slightly. Transfer the contents of the pan, oil and all, to a food processor and mince. Scrape down the sides of the bowl and add the vinegar. Whirl again in the food processor until a fine paste is achieved. Transfer the contents to a bowl, and set aside half of it. With a sharp knife, make a few gashes on each piece of chicken and add to the remaining half of the marinade mixture; toss well to coat. Cover and refrigerate overnight. Grill the chicken pieces, covered, on medium-low heat and turn occasionally to cook evenly. When the chicken is cooked through (about 20 to 25 minutes), turn up the heat slightly and char lightly for a few minutes more. Put the grilled chicken in the reserved half of the marinade and toss thoroughly to coat. Serve warm.

Chili Chicken

Chicken marinated in green chilies and tamarind

Some of the spiciest dishes in Indian cuisine come from the state of Andhra Pradesh. People there have a reputation for being able to tolerate fiery food. The reputation is well earned, as demonstrated by a friend from Andhra who entered a jalapeño pepper–eating contest in Tennessee. He won effortlessly and was still munching away long after the rest of the field had retired. This chili chicken recipe is one of my favorites; I often ate it at a famous Andhra restaurant in Bangalore where the waiter would always leave a large pitcher of cold water on the table in anticipation of the spicy food. Here I have adapted the recipe to the grill. The dish doesn't have to be unbearably hot to be enjoyed; you can temper the amount of chilies and black pepper. A raita (yogurt relish) and lots of cold water to drink on the side are absolute musts.

2 tablespoons vegetable oil

1 teaspoon black mustard seeds

¼ teaspoon fenugreek seeds

15–20 curry leaves, preferably fresh

2 medium onions, peeled and coarsely chopped

1 -inch piece of ginger, peeled and coarsely chopped

4 cloves of garlic, peeled and coarsely chopped

4 green chilies, coarsely chopped

Salt to taste

1 teaspoon ground black pepper

½ teaspoon turmeric

½ teaspoon ground coriander seeds

A lime-sized ball of seedless tamarind (4 oz.), soaked in ½ cup hot water for at least 1 hour (it should soften and absorb most of the water), *or*

2 tablespoons tamarind paste, dissolved in 4 tablespoons of water

½ cup fresh coriander leaves, chopped

2 lb. chicken, drumsticks and/or thighs, skinned, washed, and dried

Lemon juice

In a skillet, heat the oil over a medium flame and add the mustard seeds, fenugreek seeds, and the curry leaves. After a few seconds, add the chopped onions, ginger, garlic, and green chilies. Sauté until lightly touched with brown, about 5 minutes. Cool slightly, then put in a food processor, oil and all. Mince well, then add the salt, pepper, turmeric, and ground coriander. Transfer the soaked tamarind to a sieve set over a bowl and squeeze out all the pulp, discarding the fibers and seeds; you should be able to extract about 2 to 3 tablespoons. Put the extract (or the tamarind paste if you are using that) into the food processor and whirl again to mix. Transfer contents to a bowl and mix in the chopped fresh coriander leaves. With a sharp knife, make a few deep gashes in each piece of chicken, then add the chicken to the bowl. Rub in the marinade well, cover, and refrigerate overnight. When ready to cook, lift the chicken out of the marinade and grill, covered, on medium-low heat, turning and basting occasionally with the leftover marinade until tender and lightly browned, about 20 to 25 minutes. Uncover the grill, turn up the heat slightly, and char for a few minutes more. Serve with a dash of lemon juice.

bharvan murgh

*Chicken thighs marinated in sour cream and spices and
stuffed with sautéed onion, mushrooms, and bread crumbs*

I have never eaten stuffed chicken thighs in India, perhaps because
boneless, skinless chicken thighs are practically impossible to find there. If you
go out to buy chicken in India, you are usually handed a whole bird rather than
the neatly packaged components available here. When I discovered boneless
chicken thighs in my grocery store in Toronto, I found that they have many uses
in Indian cuisine. They work especially well on the grill and can be stuffed in
many different ways. In this recipe, I first marinate them in spicy sour cream and
then stuff them with sautéed mushrooms. You can vary the filling according to
choice: spiced mixed vegetables, crumbled paneer (cottage cheese), even cooked
ground lamb or beef can be substituted. Hare Aam ki Chatni (roasted green
mango chutney with fresh herbs, chilies, and garlic, page 44) served as a dip or
poured over the chicken is a wonderful complement to this dish.

For the marinade:

- 4 cloves of garlic, peeled
- 1 -inch piece of ginger, peeled
- 4 tablespoons sour cream
- 2 tablespoons grated cheddar cheese
- 1 tablespoon chickpea flour (besan) *or* 1 tablespoon white flour
- Salt to taste
- ½ teaspoon ground black pepper
- 1 teaspoon ground coriander seeds
- 1 teaspoon ground cumin seeds
- 1 teaspoon garam masala
- 2 tablespoons fresh coriander leaves
- 1½ lb. boneless, skinless chicken thighs, washed and dried

For the stuffing:

- 2 tablespoons vegetable oil
- ½ teaspoon cumin seeds
- 1 medium onion, peeled and finely chopped
- 10 medium white mushrooms, washed and finely chopped
- Salt to taste
- ½ teaspoon ground black pepper
- 2 hard-boiled eggs, peeled and mashed
- ½ cup bread crumbs
- 1 tablespoon fresh coriander leaves
- Lemon juice

In a food processor or blender, blend all marinade ingredients—except the chicken—to a smooth purée. Put the chicken in a deep bowl and pour the marinade all over, tossing to coat well. Cover and refrigerate for at least 4 hours or, preferably, overnight.

To prepare the stuffing, in a skillet, heat the oil over a medium flame and add the cumin seeds. After a few seconds, add the chopped onion. Sauté for about 5 minutes, or until lightly browned. Add the chopped mushrooms and sauté for 2 minutes, just until they begin to release their liquid. Add salt and pepper and remove the pan from the heat. Add the eggs, bread crumbs and fresh coriander to the onions and mushrooms. Stir well to mix and set aside until needed.

When you are ready to grill, lift the chicken thighs out of the marinade. Unroll one at a time on a work surface and put about a teaspoon of stuffing in the center. Roll the flap over the stuffing and secure it with 2 to 3 toothpicks. Stuff all the chicken thighs this way. Put them on a medium-hot barbecue and cook, covered, until almost done (about 20 minutes), turning the pieces only once. Uncover and let them brown slightly, taking care not to handle the pieces too much. Transfer to a platter and remove the toothpicks from the chicken. Serve with a sprinkle of lemon juice if desired.

lamb

Methiwala Gosht *Skewers of ground lamb flavored with dried fenugreek leaves and spices* **Badaami Seekh Kabobs** *Skewers of ground lamb marinated with fried onions and almonds* **Saag Seekh Kabobs** *Skewered lamb kabobs ground with spinach and spices* **Chatniwale Seekh Kabobs** *Skewers of ground lamb marinated with fresh herbs* **Achari Kabobs** *Lamb marinated in pickling spices, onions, and vinegar* **Thenga Erachi** *Lamb marinated in coconut, tamarind, and spices* **Gosht Roghan Josh** *Lamb marinated in yogurt, almonds, and ground fennel seeds* **Kathi Kabobs** *Ground meat kabobs wrapped in tortillas and grilled* **Gosht Lajawab** *Lamb marinated in onion, fenugreek, and spices* **Gosht Awadh** *Lamb marinated with sautéed onions, yogurt, spices, and fennel seeds*

*I*f you order "mutton" in a restaurant in India, you might learn the hard way that the word "mutton" can mean either lamb or goat meat. Goat is cheaper than lamb, or even chicken, and is much more common. I was surprised to find that most Westerners regard goat meat as unpalatable. Like most Indians, I prefer goat to lamb and missed eating it when I left India. It was not until I moved to Toronto that I finally managed to find some, though considerably more than I had bargained for! A friend discovered a farm that would sell him an entire goat, and he needed someone to share it with, so I became the owner of half a goat that occupied most of my freezer for the better part of a year.

Be it lamb or goat, mutton is at its finest when cooked Moghlai style. Lavishly prepared, rich with nuts and cream, it is served in literally hundreds of ways. Over the centuries, northern India's culture, religion, and geography have allied to make mutton the meat of choice. Of the two dominant religious groups, Muslims are forbidden to eat pork and Hindus eat no beef. Far from coastal waters, little seafood was available. All the creativity of Moghul cooks was focused on mutton. When I read descriptions of Moghul banquets, I am amazed at the elaborate lengths the cooks went to, sometimes roasting entire sheep stuffed with chicken, eggs, rice, nuts, and raisins. I would love to try out some of these dishes but am daunted by the thought of preparing them without a palace kitchen and an army of helpers!

Mutton is just as prominent in tandoori cooking. Cubes of mutton are grilled to make boti kabobs; ground mutton is shaped into sausage-like rolls on skewers to make seekh kabobs. Endless variations of these two preparations are possible by combining them with other ingredients and varying the spicing. In this chapter, you will find not only a variety of kabobs, but also other traditional mutton dishes that I have adapted to the grill. I use lamb in all of the following recipes, but you can substitute beef, pork, or even chicken; just adjust the cooking times accordingly. Goat meat is now available in some Indian and Caribbean grocery stores, and if you are feeling adventurous you might want to try some.

Some of the recipes use a portion of the marinade as a sauce in which to serve the grilled lamb, which makes the dish more flavorful. You can prepare these dishes up to 2 days before you plan to serve them, which allows the flavors to blend. Indians like their meat very tender, which is why I microwave the lamb before putting it on the grill. This cuts down on cooking time and also leaves the meat succulent. If you prefer your meat rare, do not microwave it before marinating.

methiwala gosht

Skewers of ground lamb flavored with dried fenugreek leaves and spices

Fenugreek is a spice you are unlikely to encounter in Western food. Indian cooks, who call it *methi*, use it in many forms. A few fenugreek seeds in hot oil add a subtle perfume to the food that is to be cooked in it. For a much more powerful impact, the seeds are powdered and sprinkled on the food as it cooks. Fresh fenugreek leaves can be cooked with potatoes or chicken, or stuffed into breads. Most versatile, however, are dried fenugreek leaves, which are prized for their distinctive aroma. Here they are blended with ground lamb, and you will experience for yourself the unique fragrance of fenugreek as the meat grills. When my husband barbecues these kabobs in our backyard, a lot of the neighborhood children (and some of their parents, too!) follow the scent and try to find excuses to drop in for a taste. For dipping, provide Mint Yogurt Dip with Roasted Garlic, page 50.

4 cloves of garlic, peeled and coarsely chopped

1 -inch piece of ginger, peeled and coarsely chopped

1 medium onion, peeled and coarsely chopped

1 large egg

Salt to taste

¼–½ teaspoon ground black pepper

1 teaspoon ground coriander seeds

1 teaspoon ground cumin seeds

1 teaspoon garam masala

¼ cup loosely packed dried fenugreek leaves

1 lb. lean ground lamb or beef

Lemon juice

SERVES 4

In a food processor, mince the garlic, ginger, and onion. Add the egg, all the spices, and the dried fenugreek leaves. Whirl once. Add the ground meat and grind until everything is well blended. Transfer the mixture to a bowl, cover, and refrigerate for 1 hour or longer. When ready to make kabobs, wet your hands lightly, shake off the excess water, and take a lemon-sized ball of the meat mixture. Mold it onto skewers in 4- to 6-inch-long sausage shapes, squeezing gently with your fingers to shape them. Grill, covered, on medium heat for about 10 minutes, turning occasionally. When the kabobs are lightly browned and cooked through, uncover the barbecue, turn up the heat to medium high, and char them lightly for a few minutes. Slide them off the skewers and onto plates, and serve them with a sprinkling of lemon juice.

badaami seekh kabobs

Skewers of ground lamb marinated with fried onions and almonds

Almonds are quite expensive in India and considered a luxury. This feeling is so deeply ingrained in me that I still treat almonds with some reverence and use them only for special occasions, such as when friends come over. The fried onions and almonds in Badaami Seekh Kabobs add a sweet flavor and make the kabobs moist and tender. You can serve them with chutney and a crunchy raita on the side. The recipe can also be halved, with smaller kabobs shaped to be served as appetizers on a bed of sliced onion and tomato rings.

2 tablespoons vegetable oil

½ teaspoon whole cumin seeds

2 medium onions, peeled and coarsely chopped

1 -inch piece of ginger, peeled and coarsely chopped

4 cloves of garlic, peeled and coarsely chopped

⅓ cup almonds, unsalted and unroasted, powdered finely

1 large egg

Salt to taste

¼–½ teaspoon ground black pepper

1 teaspoon ground cumin seeds

1 teaspoon ground coriander seeds

1 teaspoon garam masala

1 lb. ground lamb or beef

Lemon juice

SERVES 4

In a skillet, heat the oil over a high flame and add the cumin seeds. After a few seconds, add the chopped onions, ginger, and garlic. Sauté for 5 minutes, stirring frequently, until they are lightly browned. Remove from heat and allow to cool slightly. Lift the onions from the oil with a slotted spoon, pat them with a paper towel to absorb some of the oil, and mince well in a food processor. Add the egg, the almond powder, and all the spices. Whirl again to mix. Now add the ground meat and grind well in the food processor. Transfer the contents of the processor to a bowl, cover, and refrigerate for at least 1 hour. When ready to grill, wet your hands lightly, shake off the excess moisture, and take a lemon-sized ball of the mixture. Mold onto skewers in sausage shapes, about 4 to 6 inches long, pressing gently with your fingers to shape. Grill, covered, on medium heat, for about 10 minutes, turning gently once in a while for evenness. Uncover the grill, turn up the heat slightly, and char for a few minutes. Slide off the skewers and serve with a sprinkle of lemon juice.

Saag Seekh kabobs

Skewered lamb kabobs ground with spinach and spices

Gazing out of the window of a train as it winds its way through Punjab, you will see, extending to the horizon, green fields of mustard topped with bright yellow flowers swaying gently in the breeze. *Saag*, which can refer to either mustard greens or spinach, is the staple food of the Punjabi farmer. A true Punjabi, though he may have left his village decades before for life in the big city, will still wax nostalgic about the taste of saag made from freshly harvested greens. Saag can be cooked by itself or it can be combined with meat, chicken, potatoes, or cubes of lightly fried cottage cheese. Here is one of the many ways in which spinach can be served with meat in authentic Punjabi style. I prefer to use fresh spinach, though you could substitute the frozen variety. Make sure you drain the spinach very well, or the meat will fall apart on the skewers. Hare Aam ki Chatni (roasted green mango chutney with fresh herbs, chilies, and roasted garlic, page 44) or a dip would go especially well as accompaniments to these kabobs.

½ lb. trimmed spinach leaves, washed

1 medium onion, peeled and coarsely chopped

4 cloves of garlic, peeled and coarsely chopped

1 -inch piece of ginger, peeled and coarsely chopped

1 large egg

1 teaspoon garam masala

1 teaspoon ground coriander seeds

1 teaspoon ground cumin seeds

Salt to taste

¼–½ teaspoon ground black pepper

1 lb. ground lamb or beef

Lemon juice

SERVES 4

Microwave the spinach on high for 5 minutes in a microwave-safe dish covered with plastic wrap (do not add water). Uncover and transfer the spinach to a colander, and set aside to drain. In a food processor, mince the onion, garlic and ginger. Scrape the sides and add the egg, garam masala, ground coriander, ground cumin, salt, and pepper. Whirl again to mix. Squeeze out all the excess liquid from the spinach with your hands or with a fork. Transfer the spinach to the food processor and add the meat. Process until everything is well blended. Transfer the contents to a bowl, cover, and refrigerate for 1 hour or longer. When ready to grill, wet your hands lightly, shake off the excess water, and take a lemon-sized ball of the ground meat mixture. Mold it onto skewers in 4- to 6-inch-long sausage shapes, pressing gently with your fingers to shape the meat. Grill, covered, on medium heat, turning occasionally, until lightly browned and cooked through, about 10 minutes. Uncover the grill, turn up the heat slightly, and char the kabobs lightly for a few minutes more. Slide off the skewers and heap onto a plate. Serve sprinkled liberally with lemon juice.

Chatniwale Seekh kabobs

Skewers of ground lamb marinated with fresh herbs

Seekh Kabobs are perhaps the best known of tandoori preparations. Well-seasoned ground meat is molded onto long metal skewers, known as *seekhs*, which are then lowered into hot tandoors. Endless variations of this traditional technique are possible, limited only by the cook's imagination. In this recipe, a fresh, green herb chutney is ground with the meat, infusing it with its aroma as it grills. You could serve this in Tamatar Kaju ka Masala (tomato sauce with cashew nuts and sour cream, page 169) for a spectacular entrée.

1 medium onion, peeled

1 -inch piece of ginger, peeled

4 cloves of garlic, peeled

1 cup loosely packed fresh coriander leaves and upper stems, washed and drained well

1 cup loosely packed fresh mint leaves, washed and drained well

1 large egg

Salt to taste

¼–½ teaspoon ground black pepper

1 teaspoon garam masala

½ teaspoon ground cumin seeds

1 teaspoon ground coriander seeds

½ teaspoon roasted ground cumin seeds

1 lb. ground lamb or beef

Lemon juice

SERVES 4

In a food processor, mince the onion, ginger, and garlic well. Add the fresh coriander, mint, egg, and all the spices. Scrape down the sides of the food processor bowl and mince well. Now add the ground meat and whirl again until everything is well mixed. Transfer the contents to a bowl, cover, and refrigerate for at least 1 hour. When ready to barbecue, wet your hands lightly, shake off the excess water, and take a lemon-sized ball of the meat mixture. Now mold it onto skewers in sausage shapes about 4 to 6 inches long, pressing gently with your fingers to shape the meat. Grill, covered, on medium heat. When the kabobs are lightly browned and cooked through (about 10 minutes), uncover the grill, turn up the heat slightly, and char them for a few minutes more. Turn occasionally to ensure even cooking. To serve, slide off the skewers, heap onto a platter, and sprinkle liberally with lemon juice.

achari kabobs

Lamb marinated in pickling spices, onions, and vinegar

A pickle to an Indian is far more than just a cucumber preserved in vinegar. Almost anything can be pickled—mangoes, limes, and mixed vegetables, or even meat, fish, and chicken. They are tossed in spices and oil and cured in the sun. In the past, making perfect pickles was always a test of skill, and buying store-made pickles was considered beneath the dignity of a good cook. Although pickles can be sweet-and-sour or hot and spicy, there are some spices that are common to most and are known as *achari masala*, or pickling spices. This mixture of spices is used in Achari Kabobs, the flavor of which is reminiscent of a good pickle.

2 tablespoons vegetable oil

¼ teaspoon onion seeds (kalonji)

¼ teaspoon fennel seeds

¼ teaspoon cumin seeds

¼ teaspoon black mustard seeds

¼ teaspoon fenugreek seeds

4 cloves of garlic, peeled and coarsely chopped

½ -inch piece of ginger, peeled and coarsely chopped

2 medium onions, peeled and coarsely chopped

Salt to taste

¼ teaspoon cayenne pepper

½ teaspoon turmeric

¼ teaspoon garam masala

⅓ cup white vinegar

½ lb. boneless lamb or beef, washed, dried and cut into 1-inch cubes

Vegetable oil for basting

SERVES 2

In a skillet, heat oil over a medium flame and put in the onion, fennel, cumin, mustard, and fenugreek seeds. After a few seconds, add the chopped garlic, ginger, and onions. Sauté for about 5 to 7 minutes, or until the edges of the onions are lightly browned. Stir in the salt, cayenne, turmeric, and garam masala and cook for 2 minutes. Transfer the contents to a food processor or blender, add the vinegar, and mince well. Empty

half of the contents into a mixing bowl and add the meat. Coat well with the marinade, cover, and refrigerate overnight or for at least 4 hours. Reserve the remaining half of the marinade. When you are ready to grill, thread the meat onto skewers and spread any remaining marinade on top (not the reserved half of the marinade). Grill, covered, on medium-low heat until done, about 10 to 15 minutes. Baste the meat with a little oil in the last 5 to 7 minutes of cooking time. To serve, slide the meat off the skewers and toss it with the reserved marinade. This dish can be made up to 2 days ahead of time and refrigerated until used.

NOTE: If you want the meat to be very tender and to grill faster, put it in a microwave-safe bowl with 1 cup of water, seal with plastic wrap, and microwave on high for about 8 minutes. Drain and toss with the marinade. Reserve the broth for another use.

Thenga Erachi

Lamb marinated in coconut, tamarind, and spices

Coconuts, which grow abundantly along the coastline of Kerala and Tamilnadu, are an integral part of life in southern India. Tender coconut water—the product of green coconuts, which are tender-fleshed with lots of liquid—is considered an appetizer, green coconut is used to make desserts, and fresh coconut is ground into innumerable curries. The outer husk is woven into coir mats, and the shells are converted into containers, decorative ornaments, and dolls. What little is left over is burnt as fuel. Coconut is used here in a spicy chutney in which meat is first marinated and then tossed after grilling. You could serve Thenga Erachi with naan, Tandoori Paneer (cottage cheese marinated in yogurt and spices, page 123), and Thayir Pachadi (cucumber with grilled potatoes, onions, and tomatoes in yogurt, page 43). For a more substantial meal, Cholam Soop (grilled corn and onion soup in a coconut and cream broth, page 23) could precede it.

1 lb. boneless lamb or beef, cut into 1-inch pieces

½ cup coconut milk, canned

½ cup water

A lime-sized ball of seedless tamarind (4 oz.), soaked in ½ cup hot water for at least 1 hour

½ cup grated fresh coconut

½ cup packed fresh coriander leaves and tender upper stems, washed and well drained

½ -inch piece of ginger

2 cloves of garlic

8–10 curry leaves, preferably fresh

1 hot green chili

Salt to taste

¼ teaspoon ground black pepper

½ teaspoon garam masala

½ teaspoon ground coriander seeds

¼ teaspoon fenugreek seeds

Put the meat, coconut milk, and ½ cup of water in a microwave-safe bowl sealed with plastic wrap and microwave on high for 10 minutes. Drain and reserve the broth for soups. Set the meat aside. Place a sieve over a bowl and squeeze the soaked tamarind through, extracting all the pulp, and discarding the fibers. In a blender, mince the grated coconut, the tamarind extract, and all the remaining ingredients to a smooth purée. Remove to a bowl. Divide this marinade in half. Reserve half and toss the pieces of meat in the other half. When you are ready to grill, thread the meat onto skewers. Spread any remaining marinade on top. Grill, covered, on medium heat, turning occasionally until lightly browned and cooked through, about 10 minutes. When the meat is done, remove it from the skewers and toss it with the reserved marinade. Serve immediately.

gosht roghan josh

Lamb marinated in yogurt, almonds, and ground fennel seeds

Roghan Josh is the best-known Kashmiri dish. Usually, fatty cuts of lamb are chosen for this dish, which are then browned and simmered in a spicy sauce. When adapting it to the grill, I prefer to remove the fat from the meat: it's healthier, grills better, and loses none of its flavor. You could serve it with Kashmiri Murgh Elaichi (chicken breast marinated with yogurt, cardamom, and fennel, page 64) and Kashmiri Murgh Chaval (rice cooked with grilled chicken and garam masala, page 159).

2 tablespoons vegetable oil

2 medium onions, peeled and coarsely chopped

½ -inch piece of ginger, peeled and coarsely chopped

15 unroasted, unsalted whole almonds

½ cup plain yogurt (not low-fat)

¼–½ teaspoon ground black pepper

1 teaspoon garam masala

1 teaspoon powdered fennel seeds

1 teaspoon ground coriander seeds

½ teaspoon paprika

Salt to taste

1 lb. boneless lamb or beef, excess fat removed and cut into ½-inch cubes, washed, and drained

Vegetable oil for basting

SERVES 4

In a skillet, heat the oil over a medium flame and add the onions, ginger, and almonds. Sauté for 5 minutes, or until the onions are lightly browned. Switch off the heat but do not remove the pan from the burner. Now add the yogurt, all the spices, and salt. Stir to mix and let the mixture cool on the stove. Once the sauce has cooled, mince finely in a food processor. Transfer the contents to a mixing bowl, reserve half of the marinade in a separate dish, and toss the pieces of meat in the remaining half. Stir well to mix, cover, and refrigerate overnight or for at least 4 hours. When ready to grill, thread the meat onto skewers and spread any remaining marinade on top (not the reserved half). Grill, covered, on medium–low heat, turning occasionally to cook evenly. Baste with oil during the last 5 minutes of cooking time. When the meat is done to your liking, slide it off the skewers and toss it with the reserved marinade. You can make this dish up to 2 days ahead of time and refrigerate it until needed. Serve hot.

NOTE: If you want the meat to be very tender and to grill faster, microwave it, covered and with 1 cup of water, for 10 minutes. Drain and put the meat in the marinade. Reserve the broth for soups.

kathi kabobs

Ground meat kabobs wrapped in tortillas and grilled

Kathi kabobs are traditionally made by wrapping kabobs in *roomali rotis*—whole wheat dough rolled into thin disks that are broiled over an upturned skillet. Watching a skilled roti maker in action is like seeing a juggler perform. He twirls the roti around on his fingertips, tossing it from hand to hand before throwing it up in the air and finally catching it. All this is done to stretch the dough to the size and thickness of a scarf (*roomal* in Hindi). Making roomali rotis at home is not for the faint of heart; I suggest using store-bought Mexican flour tortillas, which make excellent substitutes. Kathi kabobs are a delicious way to use leftover grilled meat or chicken and are perfect for a quick lunch.

8 store-bought Mexican flour tortillas

8 or more chicken or lamb ground-meat kabobs

2 tablespoons melted butter for basting

SERVES 4

Put a tortilla on a plate and place a kabob or two in its center. Fold the two ends of the tortilla over the kabob and roll up the sides of the tortilla tightly around it, as with a Mexican burrito. Secure the flap with a toothpick. Proceed similarly with the remaining tortillas and kabobs. Place the stuffed tortillas on an open barbecue at medium-high heat and brush lightly all over with butter. When the underside of the roll is lightly browned and slightly crisp, flip it over and cook similarly on the other side. Slide onto plates and serve with chutney or dip.

gosht lajawab

Lamb marinated with onion, fenugreek, and spices.

Cubed boneless lamb is known as *boti* in Hindi. In traditional boti kabobs, the meat is first marinated in yogurt and spices, and then skewered and roasted in a tandoor. In this slight variation of the original boti kabob recipe, onions and dried fenugreek leaves have been added, giving the meat a delicious aroma on the grill. Gosht Lajawab can be served drizzled with a raita and wrapped in a warm naan. If you happen to have any leftovers, be sure to serve them in Tamatar Methi ka Masala (tomato sauce with fenugreek and cream, page 168), over a mound of steaming rice.

1 medium onion, peeled and coarsely chopped

1 -inch piece of ginger, peeled and coarsely chopped

4 cloves of garlic, peeled and coarsely chopped

¾ cup plain yogurt (not low-fat)

2 tablespoons dried fenugreek leaves

Salt to taste

¼–½ teaspoon ground black pepper

1 teaspoon garam masala

1 teaspoon ground coriander seeds

1 teaspoon ground cumin seeds

1½ lb. boneless lamb or beef, excess fat removed, cut into 1-inch cubes, washed and drained

Vegetable oil for basting (optional)

Lemon juice

In a food processor, finely mince the onion, ginger, and garlic, scraping down the sides once. Add the yogurt, fenugreek leaves, salt, pepper, garam masala, ground coriander seeds, and ground cumin seeds. Whirl to mix. Transfer the contents of the food processor to a bowl and add the meat cubes to it, tossing to coat well with the marinade. Cover and refrigerate overnight. When ready to grill, lift the meat out of the marinade and thread onto skewers. Grill, covered, on medium-low heat, turning and basting occasionally with the leftover marinade until lightly browned and cooked through, about 15 minutes. Uncover the grill, turn up the heat slightly, and char the meat lightly for a few minutes more, basting with a little vegetable oil during the last 5 to 7 minutes of cooking time to prevent them from drying out. To serve, slide them off the skewers onto a plate and sprinkle liberally with lemon juice.

NOTE: If you want the meat to be very tender and to grill faster, microwave it, covered and with 1 cup of water, for 10 minutes before putting it in the marinade. Reserve the broth for soups.

gosht awadh

Lamb marinated with sautéed onions, yogurt, spices, and fennel seeds

As the Moghul Empire declined in the eighteenth century, its outlying provinces broke away into independent principalities. The best known of these was the kingdom of Awadh, whose splendor briefly outshone even the Moghuls'. The Nawabs of Awadh were great patrons of music, art, and architecture, and they transformed the capital city of Lucknow into a glittering monument to their reign. They were also famous for giving lavish banquets for which the palace chefs constantly created new and exotic dishes. A favorite garnish was gold or silver leaf, in which individual pieces of meat were wrapped. Awadhi cuisine reflects its lavish origins in its use of extravagant ingredients, its rich flavors, and its intricate balance of spices. This recipe captures the essence of Awadhi cooking while dispensing with the gold leaf, which you are unlikely to find in your grocery store!

For the marinade:

- 2 tablespoons vegetable oil
- 2 medium onions, peeled and coarsely chopped
- 2 cloves of garlic, peeled and coarsely chopped
- 1 -inch piece of ginger, peeled and coarsely chopped
- 4 tablespoons plain yogurt (not low-fat)
- Salt to taste
- ½ teaspoon ground black pepper
- 1 teaspoon garam masala
- 1 teaspoon ground coriander seeds
- ¾ teaspoon ground cumin seeds
- ½ teaspoon turmeric
- 1 teaspoon ground fennel seeds
- ¼ teaspoon carom seeds (ajwain), optional
- 1 lb. boned and defatted lamb or beef, cut into 1-inch pieces
- Vegetable oil for basting

For the finishing:

- 2 tablespoons heavy cream
- ¼ teaspoon garam masala
- ½ teaspoon dried and powdered mint leaves, optional

In a skillet, heat the oil over a medium flame and add the onions. Sauté them, stirring occasionally, until lightly browned, about 5 to 7 minutes. Lift them out of the oil with a slotted spoon and cool to room temperature. Put the onions in a food processor or blender and add all the remaining ingredients for the marinade except the meat and vegetable oil. Process until well blended, then transfer half the contents of the processor to a mixing bowl. Reserve the other half in the refrigerator. Toss the meat into the mixing bowl, coat well with the marinade, cover, and refrigerate overnight, or for at least 4 hours. When ready to grill, thread the meat onto skewers and spread any remaining marinade on top. Grill, covered, on medium-low heat until done to your liking, about 15 minutes. Keep turning the skewers occasionally, checking to see if they are done. During the last 5 minutes of cooking time, brush the meat lightly with oil to prevent it from drying out. While the meat is grilling, cook the remaining marinade for 5 minutes on medium-low heat, then mix in the cream, garam masala, and mint leaves. Remove the meat from the skewers and toss gently with the sauce. The entire dish can be made up to 2 days ahead of time and reheated gently before serving.

NOTE: If you want the meat to be very tender and to cook faster, microwave it, covered and with 1 cup of water for 10 minutes before putting it in the marinade. Reserve the broth for another use.

Seafood

Machali Masala *Grilled breaded salmon steaks marinated in olive oil, lemon juice, herbs, and spices* **Tandoori Machali** *Fish fillet marinated in sour cream and spices* **Hari Machali** *Fish steaks marinated in fresh coriander, dried fenugreek leaves, and spices* **Sorse Maach** *Fish fillet marinated and served in a sauce of ground mustard seeds, spices, yogurt, onion, and tomatoes* **Sindhi Hariyali Machali** *Salmon steaks marinated in lemon juice and spices, served in a sauce of sautéed onion, fresh coriander, and tomatoes* **Imliwali Machali** *Fish steaks marinated in tamarind and toasted ground spices* **Thenga Meen** *Fish fillet marinated with lemon juice and spices, served in a sauce of sautéed onion, coconut, tomato, and spices* **Patra ni Machali** *Fish steaks coated with a sauce of coconut, fresh coriander, and spices* **Jhinga Moongphaliwala** *Shrimp marinated with ground roasted peanuts, yogurt, and spices, and skewered with tomatoes* **Jhinga Patia** *Sweet, hot, and sour shrimp marinated and served in a sauce of onion, tomato, spices, and tamarind* **Tandoori Jhinga** *Shrimp marinated in thickened yogurt and spices, lightly breaded, and grilled with onion*

the best tandoori fish I ever ate was, oddly enough, not in India. Years ago, my husband and I were in London, traveling on a graduate student's shoestring budget. We were walking down Oxford Street, trying to decide where to eat, when we ran into an old family friend. To our delight she invited us to dine with her at a posh Indian restaurant, where I ate tandoori trout for the first time. After all these years I still recall it as the most delectable fish I have ever had.

It is not surprising that I had never eaten tandoori seafood while living in Delhi. Living far from the ocean, the Moghuls had no tradition of cooking seafood, and it is only in recent years that creative cooks have adopted tandoori cooking techniques for preparing seafood. Now you find everything from trout to lobster being lowered into the tandoor, and fish tikkas (boneless fish chunks marinated in spices and grilled) are all the rage in Delhi.

To find the best seafood cooked in the traditional way, you have to travel to India's coasts. Fishing is a way of life along the shores of the Indian Ocean, and the people make full use of the abundant seafood. In Kerala, fish is cooked with coconut milk to make *molee*. The Parsis of Bombay prepare *patra ni machali* by coating fish with spicy chutney and wrapping it in banana leaves. Bengalis cook fish in a pungent mustard paste to make *sorse maach*. Bengalis are so fond of fish that even orthodox Brahmins, who consider themselves vegetarians, will eat it, calling it "fruit of the sea."

In this chapter, I present tandoori and other ways to cook seafood on the grill. Some of the recipes are traditional, others are ones that I have created based on the cooking styles of different regions of India. In some of the recipes, the fish is served in a sauce, which I recommend preparing ahead of time. If you like fillets better than steaks, by all means substitute them.

machali masala

Grilled breaded salmon steaks marinated in olive oil,
lemon juice, herbs, and spices

On a recent family camping trip to Tobermory, Ontario, we had the local specialty—fresh whitefish fillets breaded and grilled on an open fire. It was a revelation to me that breaded fish could be grilled at all, let alone so superbly. When I came home, I just had to try out the recipe—Indian style. I use salmon steaks here, but you could substitute the fish of your choice. The breaded exterior makes the fish nice and crispy, keeping it moist inside. I spice the dish very lightly, so as not to overpower the fish's delicate flavor. This recipe goes especially well with Roasted Red Pepper and Garlic Yogurt Dip (page 51) on the side, and with Bhutte ka Salat (grilled corn and roasted red peppers tossed with onions in a lemon and roasted-spice dressing, page 29).

2 slices of white bread

¼ cup olive oil

1 clove of garlic, peeled and grated

Salt to taste

¼–½ teaspoon ground black pepper

¼ teaspoon ground coriander seeds

¼ teaspoon ground cumin seeds

¼ teaspoon garam masala

2 tablespoons finely chopped fresh coriander leaves

1 lb. salmon steaks (approx. 4 small), washed and dried

Lemon juice

SERVES 4

Put the slices of bread on a paper towel and microwave on high for 1 minute per side. Cool and put in a food processor. Crumble to fine crumbs. Transfer to a bowl and set aside. Put the olive oil in a bowl and add the garlic as well as all the remaining ingredients except the lemon juice and bread crumbs. Mix well, then rub all over the salmon steaks. Cover and refrigerate for an hour or longer. When ready to grill, sprinkle half the bread crumbs on top of the steaks, pat lightly with your fingertips to keep them in place, and place the steaks crumb side down on the grill. Sprinkle the remaining bread crumbs on the other side and pat them down again. Grill, covered, on medium heat for about 7 minutes. When the bottom is lightly browned and crisp, flip the steaks over and cook similarly on the other side. Slide onto plates and douse liberally with lemon juice or serve with a wedge of lemon on the side.

Tandoori machali

Fish fillet marinated in sour cream and spices

If you want to eat Tandoori Machali the traditional way, try serving the fish whole. In India, the marinated fish is skewered from mouth to tail and lowered into the tandoor to grill. If, however, having the fish looking back at you while you eat makes you nervous, use the fillet as given in the recipe below.

2 cloves of garlic, peeled and grated

2 tablespoons fresh coriander leaves, chopped

2 tablespoons sour cream

Salt to taste

¼–½ teaspoon ground black pepper

½ teaspoon garam masala

¼ teaspoon ground coriander seeds

¼ teaspoon ground cumin seeds

1 tablespoon dried fenugreek leaves

1 lb. fish fillet, such as salmon, washed and dried

Lemon juice

SERVES 4

In a mixing bowl, combine all ingredients except the fish and lemon juice. Mix well, then rub this marinade all over the fish except the skin side. Allow to marinate for half an hour. When ready to grill, place the fillet, skin side down, in a covered barbecue and cook on medium heat until done, about 7 minutes. Flip it over carefully and cook the marinated side until lightly browned and cooked through, another 5 to 7 minutes. Avoid flipping repeatedly, as it may fall apart. Remove to a platter and sprinkle with lemon juice.

hari machali

Fish steaks marinated in fresh coriander, dried fenugreek leaves, and spices

Smothered in a fresh green herb sauce, this fish smells delicious as it grills. The marinade is simple and easy to prepare—you only have to throw the ingredients in the blender and you're nearly done. Serve with Murgh Kasoori (skewers of ground chicken marinated with fried onion and dried fenugreek leaves, page 58) and naan.

1 clove of garlic, peeled

½ -inch piece of ginger, peeled

1 hot green chili

½ cup packed fresh coriander leaves and tender upper stems, washed and drained well

3 tablespoons lemon juice

2 tablespoons olive oil

Salt to taste

¼–½ teaspoon ground black pepper

¼ teaspoon garam masala

¼ teaspoon turmeric

2 tablespoons dried fenugreek leaves

1 lb. white-fleshed fish steak—such as haddock, halibut, or cod— washed and dried

1 lemon

SERVES 4

In a blender, purée all ingredients (except the fish) to a smooth paste. Transfer to a bowl. Rub this paste all over the fish on both sides. Cover and marinate for at least an hour in the refrigerator. When ready to grill, cook the steaks in a covered grill at medium heat until lightly browned and charred in places, about 8 to 10 minutes per side. Flip the steaks just once during cooking to prevent them from falling apart. Slide onto plates and serve with a wedge of lemon on the side.

Sorse Maach

Fish fillet marinated and served in a sauce of ground
mustard seeds, spices, yogurt, onion, and tomatoes

The landscape of Bengal is crisscrossed by seemingly endless rivers and streams that feed the Ganges River on its way to the Bay of Bengal. The multitude of fish caught in these waters are used in many creative ways by Bengali cooks. Most dishes are seasoned with *panchphoran* (literally, "five spices"), a combination of fennel, onion, cumin, mustard, and fenugreek seeds. Mustard oil, with its pungent aroma and flavor, is the preferred medium of cooking in this region. Sorse Maach is a good example of Bengali cuisine. Grilling the fish before putting it into the sauce, as I do here, makes the dish more sumptuous. Rice, which soaks up the fiery sauce, is often served as an accompaniment to fish dishes.

2 cloves of garlic, peeled and coarsely chopped

½ -inch piece of ginger, peeled and coarsely chopped

1 small onion, peeled and coarsely chopped

1 hot green chili, stemmed and coarsely chopped

1 small tomato, coarsely chopped

¼ teaspoon cumin seeds, powdered

¼ teaspoon onion seeds (kalonji), powdered

1½ teaspoons black mustard seeds, powdered

¼ teaspoon fenugreek seeds, powdered

½ teaspoon ground coriander seeds

½ teaspoon garam masala

Salt to taste

½ teaspoon turmeric

2 tablespoons vegetable oil

2 tablespoons plain yogurt

1 lb. white-fleshed fish fillet

Lemon juice

SERVES 4

In a food processor or blender, mince garlic, ginger, onion, chili, and tomato well. Add the powdered cumin, onion seeds, mustard seeds, and fenugreek seeds to the minced onions along with the ground coriander, garam masala, salt, and turmeric. Mix well. In a skillet, heat the oil over a medium-high flame and add the ground onion and spice mixture. Stirring frequently, cook for about 5 to 8 minutes, or until the raw smell has dissipated. Switch off the heat, but let the pan remain on the stove. Add the yogurt and stir well. Let the marinade cool to room temperature on the stove. When ready to grill, spread about 2 to 3 tablespoons of this marinade over the meat side of the fillet. Reserve the remaining marinade. Place the fillet skin side down in a covered grill over medium heat. Grill until cooked through and lightly charred, about 8 to 10 minutes per side, flipping the fish once to cook on the other side. To serve, spoon the remaining sauce over the fish and sprinkle with some lemon juice. Variation: Instead of spooning the sauce over the fish, you can also skin the fillet, divide the fish into chunks, and then toss them into the reserved sauce.

sindhi hariyali machali

Salmon steaks marinated in lemon juice and spices, served in a sauce of sautéed onion, fresh coriander, and tomatoes

During my visits to India, my parents' neighbor Roma Ramchandani—a Sindhi cook par excellence—always sends samples of her choice dishes so I can have a taste of true Sindhi food. I fondly remember a wonderful recipe of fish cooked in a green herb sauce that she sent around for me to try. Her recipe calls for the fish to be braised in the herb sauce, but it cooks equally well on the grill. Here, the fish is marinated in lemon juice and spices and then tossed in a sautéed herb sauce. When served with naan, this makes a delicious meal.

For the marinade:

Salt to taste

½ teaspoon turmeric

2 tablespoons lemon juice

¼–½ teaspoon ground black pepper

1 lb. salmon steaks (about 3–4 medium), washed and dried

For the sauce:

1 medium onion, peeled

2 cloves of garlic, peeled

½ -inch piece of ginger, peeled

1 cup packed fresh coriander leaves and upper stems, washed and drained

3 tablespoons vegetable oil

½ teaspoon cumin seeds

½ cup diced plum tomatoes (fresh or canned)

Salt to taste

¼ teaspoon turmeric

¼ teaspoon cayenne pepper (optional)

¼ teaspoon garam masala

¼ teaspoon ground coriander seeds

2 tablespoons plain low-fat yogurt

¼ cup water

Make a paste of all the marinade ingredients and spoon it generously on both sides of the steaks. Marinate, covered, for about half an hour or refrigerate for longer. Meanwhile, prepare the sauce. In a food processor or blender, mince the onion, garlic, and ginger well, then add the fresh coriander and mince again until fairly smooth. In a skillet, heat the oil over a medium-high flame. Add the cumin seeds and, after a few seconds, add the minced onions from the blender. Sauté, stirring frequently for about 8 minutes, until the onions are lightly browned and the raw smell has dissipated. Whirl the tomatoes in the blender or food processor and add them to the onions in the pan. Cook until the moisture has evaporated and they have thickened slightly, about 5 to 7 minutes. Add all the spices and cook for another 2 minutes. Reduce heat to low, beat the yogurt with a spoon for a few seconds, and add to the onion-tomato mixture, stirring all the while to incorporate it into the sauce. Cook for 5 minutes, stirring frequently, then add the water. Turn off the heat and let the pan sit on the hot stove. The sauce is now ready and can be prepared and refrigerated up to 2 days in advance.

When you are ready to grill, lift the fish steaks out of the marinade and grill, covered, over medium heat, turning once. They should be lightly browned and cooked through when done, which will take about 5 to 7 minutes for each side.

Remove them to a plate and take off the skin and bones, dividing the fish into chunks as you do so. Put the chunks into the sauce and warm the sauce over a medium heat, stirring very gently so as not to break up the fish.

imliwali machali

Fish steaks marinated in tamarind and toasted ground spices

A tamarind tree is the best play area a child can ask for. Its thick low branches are perfect for climbing and for building tree houses, its dense foliage provides shade, and when hunger pangs strike, all you have to do is reach out and pluck the fruit. Generations of children have been warned not to eat tamarind because it will make them sick, but they do it anyway. The fruit of the tamarind tree, which looks much like a fat green bean when it is unripe, is used for pickling and chutneys. It ripens to a chocolate brown color and is extremely sour. The extract from the ripe tamarind is used in cooking sauces and chutneys and is valued for its unique flavor. In Indian grocery stores you'll usually find peeled, seedless tamarind or tamarind paste.

¼ teaspoon fenugreek seeds

1 teaspoon whole coriander seeds

1 teaspoon fennel seeds

½ teaspoon cumin seeds

2 whole cloves

2 green cardamom

½ -inch stick cinnamon

½ teaspoon whole black pepper

Salt to taste

½ -inch piece of ginger, peeled and grated

2 cloves of garlic, peeled and grated

1 tablespoon vegetable oil

A lime-sized piece of seedless tamarind (4 oz.), soaked in ½ cup hot water for at least 1 hour and mashed with a fork

1 lb. fish steaks

In a skillet over medium heat, combine the fenugreek, coriander, fennel, and cumin seeds, cloves, cardamom, cinnamon, and black pepper. Toast them for a few minutes until they darken and smell roasted. Cool and transfer to a clean coffee or spice grinder. Powder finely. Remove to a bowl and mix in the salt. Add the ginger and garlic to the spices, along with the oil. Transfer the soaked tamarind to a sieve over a bowl and squeeze out all the pulp with your hands, discarding the fibers. Put the tamarind extract into the bowl with the powdered spices and mix everything well with a spoon. Rub this paste all over the fish. Marinate for 1 hour or longer in the refrigerator. Grill the fish in a covered barbecue at medium heat. After 5 to 7 minutes, flip the fish and cook on the other side for the same length of time. To check doneness, poke it with a fork to see if it flakes easily. Serve hot.

Thenga Meen

*Fish fillet marinated in lemon juice and spices, served in
a sauce of sautéed onion, coconut, tomato, and spices*

The fifteenth-century European explorers who set sail for the
fabled Malabar Coast in search of riches found little treasure, but the pepper,
cloves, and cardamom they brought back from India sold for their weight in
gold. In Kerala, the state in which Malabar lies, almost every house has spices
growing in its garden. When I lived there, we had green cardamom and black
pepper growing in our backyard, and my mother would pluck them fresh to use
in her cooking. Kerala cuisine uses coconut and spices liberally, as you will discover from this recipe. Thenga Meen is usually served with rice.

1 lb. fish fillet, such as salmon, washed and dried

For the marinade:

1 tablespoon lemon juice

½ teaspoon salt

½ teaspoon turmeric

For the sauce:

2 cloves of garlic, peeled

½ -inch piece of ginger, peeled

2 tablespoons fresh grated coconut

1 large tomato, coarsely chopped

2 tablespoons vegetable oil

¼ teaspoon fenugreek seeds

½ teaspoon black mustard seeds

10 curry leaves, preferably fresh

1 small onion, peeled and finely chopped

½ teaspoon ground coriander seeds

½ teaspoon ground cumin seeds

¼–½ teaspoon freshly cracked black pepper

Salt to taste (optional)

A lime-sized piece of seedless tamarind (4 oz.), soaked in ½ cup hot water for at least 1 hour *or*

2 tablespoons tamarind paste dissolved in 4 tablespoons hot water

Make a paste with the lemon juice, salt, and turmeric and rub it all over the fish. Set aside to marinate. In a food processor, mince the garlic, ginger, coconut, and tomato finely. In a skillet, heat the oil over a medium flame and put in the fenugreek seeds, black mustard seeds, and curry leaves. As soon as they begin to splutter, add the onion. Sauté for about 5 minutes or until lightly browned, then add the ground coriander, ground cumin, black pepper, and salt, if desired. Add the coconut paste from the food processor and cook for about 2 to 3 minutes, or until the liquid has evaporated. Meanwhile, transfer the soaked tamarind to a sieve set over a bowl and squeeze the pulp through and discard the fibers. Add the extract to the onion-coconut mixture and cook for another 2 minutes, or until the sauce is fairly thick. Switch off the heat and let the pan sit on the stove to keep the sauce warm. This sauce can be made up to 2 days ahead of time if kept refrigerated. When ready to cook, lift the fish out of its marinade and grill it, covered, skin side down. Cook on medium heat until done on one side, about 5 to 7 minutes. Flip carefully and cook on the other side for another 5 to 7 minutes. When cooked through, flip onto a plate skin side down and spoon the sauce on top. You can also skin the fish, divide it into chunks, and toss it gently with the sauce.

patra ni machali

Fish steaks coated with a sauce of coconut, fresh coriander, and spices

Parsis, a community in India, always serve this dish at weddings and special occasions. The secret to great taste is to use fresh sweet coconut. When you are buying it, look at the "eyes"—the depressions at the top of the coconut—which should be clean and brown and not covered with mold. Shake the coconut and listen for the slosh of the water inside. If you don't hear it, choose another one. You could serve this dish with rice and a soup such as the Mili Juli Sabzi ka Shorva (grilled mixed vegetable soup in chicken broth, page 25).

2 tablespoons vinegar

½ teaspoon turmeric

½ teaspoon salt

1¼ lb. white-fleshed fish steak, such as halibut or haddock, washed and dried

2 cloves of garlic, peeled

½ -inch piece of ginger, peeled

1 cup grated fresh coconut

1 hot green chili

10 curry leaves (optional)

1 cup packed fresh coriander leaves and tender upper stems, washed and drained well

Salt to taste

½ teaspoon ground coriander seeds

½ teaspoon ground cumin seeds

1 teaspoon sugar

2 tablespoons lemon juice

Additional fresh-squeezed lime juice, if needed

SERVES 4

Combine the vinegar, turmeric, and ½ teaspoon of salt and rub it all over the fish. Cover and set the fish aside. Combine the garlic, ginger, coconut, green chili, curry leaves, fresh coriander, salt, ground coriander, cumin, sugar, and lemon juice in a blender and blend to a smooth paste, adding 2 or more spoonfuls of water if necessary. Transfer the contents to a bowl. Spread half of this paste over one side of the fish steak. Cut a piece of aluminum foil large enough to fully wrap each fish steak and lay the fish sauce side down on the foil. Spread the remaining sauce over the other side of the steak and wrap it in the foil tightly, like an envelope. Repeat similarly for all the fish steaks. Cook the foiled-covered fish on a medium-hot, covered grill for about

15 minutes, turning them occasionally. To check doneness, loosen one part of the foil to see if the fish flakes easily. Remove the fish gently from its foil packet. Slide them onto plates and smooth the sauce from the foil onto the fish. Serve with an additional squeeze of lime juice or with wedges of lime on the side.

Jhinga moongphaliwala

Shrimp marinated with ground roasted peanuts, yogurt, and spices, and skewered with tomatoes

In winter, when peanuts are in season, you can smell the delicious aroma of roasting peanuts in every marketplace and street corner of India. You warm your hands in front of the fire while the peanut seller roasts the peanuts in a wok placed over a charcoal stove. He tosses them with a little salt, deftly wraps them in a paper cone, and sells them to you for a few coins. The crunch of the roasted peanuts nicely complements the succulent shrimp in this recipe, while the grilled tomatoes add substance.

½ -inch piece of ginger, peeled

2 cloves of garlic, peeled

¼ cup roasted peanuts

2 tablespoons plain yogurt (not low-fat)

Salt to taste

¼–½ teaspoon ground black pepper

½ teaspoon garam masala

4 Italian plum tomatoes

½ lb. uncooked, unpeeled shrimp, fresh or frozen, peeled, deveined, washed and drained

Lemon juice

SERVES 4

In a food processor, mince the ginger and garlic. Add the peanuts and mince again until the mixture resembles bread crumbs. Transfer to a bowl and add all the remaining ingredients except the tomatoes and lemon juice. Mix well, then add the shrimp. Toss to coat with the marinade, cover, and set aside in the refrigerator for at least 4 hours. When ready to grill, quarter the tomatoes and skewer them, alternating with the shrimp. Spread any remaining marinade on top of the skewers. Grill, covered, on a medium flame for about 5 to 7 minutes on each side, or until the shrimp are cooked and lightly charred. When cool enough to handle, slide the shrimp and tomatoes off of the skewers, heap them in a platter, and toss them with the lemon juice.

Jhinga patia

Sweet, hot, and sour shrimp marinated and served in a
sauce of onion, tomato, spices, and tamarind

Parsis came to settle in Gujarat in the eighth century, escaping religious persecution in Iran. The king of Gujarat gave them freedom to practice their Zoroastrian religion but decreed their adoption of the local language and mode of dress. They prospered as merchants over the years and to this day maintain their unique customs and religion. They have a very distinctive style of cooking that has evolved as a mixture of Iranian, Gujarati, and English styles. Their food often mixes sweet, sour, and spicy flavors, and combines dried fruits and nuts with meats, fish, and vegetables to make delicious curries, chutneys, and pickles. Jhinga Patia is traditionally served with rice on special occasions.

2 tablespoons
vegetable oil

½ teaspoon cumin
seeds

1 medium onion,
peeled and
coarsely chopped

2 cloves of garlic,
peeled and
coarsely chopped

2 hot green chilies,
chopped

10–15 curry leaves,
fresh or dried

1 medium tomato,
chopped

2 teaspoons sugar

½ teaspoon ground
coriander seeds

½ teaspoon ground
cumin seeds

½ teaspoon
turmeric

Salt to taste

½ teaspoon garam
masala

1 lime-sized ball
of seedless
tamarind,
(4 oz.), soaked in
½ cup hot water
for at least
1 hour, and
mashed with
a fork or
2 tablespoons
tamarind paste
dissolved in
4 tablespoons
of water

2 tablespoons
chopped fresh
coriander leaves

½ lb. uncooked
shrimp, fresh or
frozen, peeled,
deveined,
washed, and
drained

Lemon juice

In a skillet, heat the oil over a medium flame and add the cumin seeds. After a few seconds, mix in the onions, garlic, green chilies, and curry leaves. Sauté for 5 minutes until the edges of the onions are lightly browned. Add the chopped tomato, sugar, ground coriander, ground cumin, turmeric, salt, and garam masala. Cook for another 2 minutes, mashing lightly with the back of a spoon. Remove from heat. Set a sieve over a bowl and empty the tamarind and its liquid into it. Using your hands, squeeze out the pulp from the tamarind and discard the fibrous residue, then add the extract to the tomato-onion mixture. If using the tamarind paste, add it now. Transfer everything to a food processor and mince well. Remove to a bowl and mix in the fresh coriander leaves. Reserve half the marinade and toss the shrimp in the remaining half, coating them well with the marinade. Cover and refrigerate for at least 4 hours or, preferably, overnight. When ready to grill, lift the shrimp out of the marinade and thread onto skewers. Grill, covered, on medium heat. When the underside is done, about 7 minutes, flip the skewers and grill for another 5 to 7 minutes. To serve, slide shrimp off the skewers and toss with the reserved marinade. Sprinkle with lemon juice if desired.

Tandoori Jhinga

Shrimp marinated in thickened yogurt and spices, lightly breaded, and grilled with onion

Shrimp is not usually breaded when cooked in a tandoor. As an experiment, I breaded some lightly before grilling and got rave reviews from my family. In this recipe, the breaded shrimp is also interspersed with onion for a tasty combination.

3 tablespoons plain yogurt (not low-fat), drained through a sieve lined with a coffee filter for 15 minutes (until thickened)

½ -inch piece of ginger, peeled and grated

2 cloves of garlic, peeled and grated

Salt to taste

¼–½ teaspoon ground black pepper

¼–½ teaspoon cayenne pepper

¼ teaspoon garam masala

¼ teaspoon ground coriander seeds

¼ teaspoon ground cumin seeds

¼ teaspoon ground roasted cumin seeds

¼ teaspoon carom seeds (ajwain), (optional)

½ lb. uncooked, unpeeled shrimp, fresh or frozen, peeled and deveined, washed and drained

1 slice of white bread

1 medium onion, peeled and chopped into 1-inch pieces

Lemon juice

SERVES 4

Place the drained and thickened yogurt into a bowl. Add the grated ginger and garlic, salt, and all the spices. Mix well, then toss in the shrimp. Cover and refrigerate for at least 4 hours. When ready to grill, make the bread crumbs. Place the bread on a paper towel and microwave on high for 1 minute on each side. Cool, then crumble in a food processor or by hand. Skewer the shrimp, alternating with the chopped onions. Lay them side by side on a plate and sprinkle half the bread crumbs on one side, patting lightly to hold them in place; flip the skewers and repeat on the other side. Grill, covered, on a medium flame for about 5 to 7 minutes on each side. When the shrimp are cooked and lightly charred, remove from the grill. Take them off the skewers, pile on a platter, and toss with the lemon juice.

Vegetables

Tandoori Paneer *Cottage cheese marinated in yogurt and spices* **bhuna baingan Masalewala** *Eggplant slices grilled with spiced oil* **Tandoori Paneer Chatniwali** *Cottage cheese marinated in fresh coriander, mint, and spices* **Chili Paneer** *Cottage cheese marinated in green chilies, ginger, garlic, fresh coriander, and soy sauce* **Kaju Methi Paneer ke Tikke** *Grilled cottage cheese and green peppers marinated and served in a sauce of cashew nuts, dried fenugreek leaves, tomatoes, and cream* **Paneer Durbari** *Grilled cottage cheese served in a tomato cream sauce with sautéed onion and green pepper* **bhune Alu Masaledaar** *Crispy potatoes marinated in spices, fresh coriander, and olive oil* **Tandoori gobhi** *Cauliflower florets marinated in yogurt and spices* **bhuna hua bhurta** *Roasted eggplant, onions, and tomatoes sautéed with spices* **baingan kashmiri** *Baby eggplant coated in a sweet-and-sour tamarind-fennel sauce served with grilled apples* **Alu Moongphali aur Paneer ke kabob** *Croquettes of mashed potatoes, cottage cheese, and roasted peanuts* **bhutte ke kabob** *Skewers of mashed potatoes and*

corn *Chane ki tikki* Croquettes of mashed chickpeas, potatoes, and spices *Alu Matar ki tikki* Croquettes of mashed potatoes stuffed with green peas, ginger, and spices *Alu bharu Simla Mirch* Green peppers stuffed with spicy sautéed potatoes *kaddoo ki Sabzi* Roasted pumpkin with onions and fenugreek seeds *bharvan guchchi* Portobello mushrooms marinated in vinegar and spices, stuffed with spiced feta cheese *guchchi ki Sabzi* Grilled mushrooms served in a sauce of sautéed onion, tomatoes, and cream

My son Rohan was 4 months old when I gave him his first taste of solid food. This is a momentous occasion for Hindus, marked by a ceremony known as *annaprashan*, which translates as "presenting of grain." I lovingly prepared the traditional dish of rice, lentils, and vegetables and gave him a spoonful before an audience of camera-toting friends and relatives. He promptly spat it all out, which rather ruined the moment!

Annaprashan celebrates the fact that the first food a Hindu tastes is grain and, for most Hindus, vegetarianism is a way of life. As a result, India has the most diverse and imaginative vegetarian cuisine in the world. There are many vegetables unique to India that I have never found elsewhere, and as far as I know they do not even have English names. There are many ways to prepare each vegetable: they can be stir-fried, served in a sauce, stuffed, minced, or grilled. Some recipes are wonderfully specialized; one of my favorites uses just the flower of the zucchini plant dipped in a light batter and deep fried into a *pakora* (dumpling); another makes a spicy dish from radish greens. A typical meal consists of a lentil dish and one or two vegetable dishes; even if meat is on the menu, a vegetable dish will accompany it.

European colonists left little lasting impact on Indian cuisine. However, they brought with them a variety of new vegetables—potatoes, tomatoes, corn, cabbage, lettuce, eggplant, and chili peppers—that Indians enthusiastically incorporated into their own food. These vegetables adapted well to local cooking techniques, and it is now hard to imagine Indian food without them.

This chapter offers many unusual ways to grill vegetables. Although tandoori food focuses on meat, I find that the same marinades can be used to cook vegetables and *paneer* (cottage cheese). Traditional vegetable recipes are usually cooked on wood or charcoal fires and can easily be prepared on a barbecue. A few of the recipes are my own creations in which I have taken some of my favorite foods, like feta cheese and sun-dried tomatoes, and combined them with Indian ingredients, producing what I hope is the best of all worlds.

Tandoori Paneer

Cottage cheese marinated in yogurt and spices

Paneer is usually referred to as cottage cheese in Indian cookbooks. This is a loose translation at best, since paneer is quite different from the cottage cheese you find in American grocery stores. Paneer is compressed cottage cheese, drained of all its whey, with a firm texture and nutty flavor. It can be cubed or grated for use in cooking. Paneer is versatile and can be used as stuffing for breads, for making *pakoras* (dumplings), or it can be lightly fried and put in a sauce. Paneer comes off the grill brown and crisp on the outside and soft and delicious on the inside. This recipe can also double as a side dish or as an entrée for vegetarians. You can serve it on a bed of crisp lettuce, layered with sliced tomatoes for an attractive hors d'œuvre. Cherry tomatoes or green peppers can also be skewered instead of, or along with, the onions.

4 cloves of garlic, peeled and minced or grated

½ -inch piece of ginger, peeled and minced or grated

½ cup plain yogurt (not low-fat)

¼ teaspoon carom seeds (ajwain), optional

Salt to taste

¼–½ teaspoon ground black pepper

1 tablespoon tomato ketchup

½ teaspoon garam masala

2 teaspoons dried fenugreek leaves

½ teaspoon ground coriander seeds

½ teaspoon ground cumin seeds

½ lb. paneer (cottage cheese), diced into 1-inch pieces

1 medium onion, peeled and cut into 1-inch chunks

Lemon juice

SERVES 4

In a bowl, combine the garlic, ginger, yogurt, carom seeds, salt, pepper, ketchup, garam masala, dried fenugreek leaves, ground coriander seeds, and the ground cumin seeds. Mix well, then add the cubes of paneer and the onion pieces. Toss well to coat, cover, and refrigerate for 1 hour or longer. When ready to grill, lift the paneer out of the marinade and thread onto skewers, alternating with the onion pieces. Grill, covered, over medium heat until lightly browned, about 10 minutes. Turn the skewers occasionally and baste with the leftover marinade. At the end of the cooking time, uncover the grill, turn up the heat slightly, and lightly char the paneer for 2 minutes more. Slide the paneer and onions off the skewers, heap onto a platter, and serve with a sprinkle of lemon juice.

bhuna baingan masalewala

Eggplant slices grilled with spiced oil

Eggplant gets its name from the white variety that does resemble an egg. This kind is rarely seen in India, and most vegetarians would be reluctant to eat anything that contains egg, even if only in name. Eggplant in India is called *baingan* in Hindi and *brinjal* in English. I had always assumed that brinjal was an English word until I discovered that no American had ever heard it. Actually it is purely an Indian creation, derived from the Portuguese word *brinjella*. This recipe is based on a common Indian dish in which the eggplant is lightly fried in oil. I find that grilling it improves the flavor of the dish.

2 medium eggplant (about 1¼ lb.), washed and dried, stemmed and sliced into ½-inch-thick rounds

⅓ cup olive oil

Salt to taste

¼–½ teaspoon ground black pepper

¼–½ teaspoon cayenne pepper

½ teaspoon garam masala

½ teaspoon roasted ground cumin seeds

½ teaspoon ground coriander seeds

½ teaspoon ground cumin seeds

1 tablespoon chopped fresh coriander leaves

Lemon juice

SERVES 4

Arrange the eggplant slices in a non-overlapping layer on a platter. In a bowl, mix the salt and all the spices into the oil. Using a pastry brush or a spoon, rub half of this spiced oil on one side of the eggplant slices. Put the slices spiced side down on a medium-hot barbecue grill and cook, uncovered, for about 7 to 8 minutes per side. While the underside is cooking, baste the top with the remaining spiced oil. When the eggplant is lightly charred and cooked through, transfer the slices carefully to a platter, sprinkle on the chopped fresh coriander and lemon juice, and serve hot.

Tandoori Paneer Chatniwali

Cottage cheese marinated in fresh coriander, mint, and spices

Marinating cubes of *paneer* (cottage cheese) in chutney not only infuses the paneer with a heady aroma, it also eliminates the need for any dip on the side. If you want the dish to have a bit of a sauce, then throw the grilled paneer back into leftover marinade—just make sure you don't use it all up for basting. For variety, you can alternate pieces of onion or peeled and diced raw mangoes with the paneer on the skewers. You could also serve Tandoori Paneer Chatniwali as an appetizer on a bed of sliced tomatoes. Leftovers make excellent vegetarian Kathi Kabobs (ground meat kabobs wrapped in tortillas and grilled, page 95).

1 medium onion, peeled and coarsely chopped

2 cloves of garlic, peeled and coarsely chopped

½ -inch piece of ginger, peeled and coarsely chopped

1½ cups loosely packed fresh coriander leaves and tender upper stems, washed and drained

1 cup loosely packed fresh mint leaves, washed and drained

1 hot green chili (optional)

4 tablespoons plain yogurt (not low-fat)

Salt to taste

¼–½ teaspoon cayenne pepper

½ teaspoon cumin seeds

¼ teaspoon black salt (optional)

½ teaspoon roasted ground cumin seeds

½ teaspoon garam masala

½ lb. paneer (cottage cheese), cut into ½ -inch cubes

Lemon juice

SERVES 4

In a food processor, mince the onion, garlic, and ginger. Add the coriander and mint leaves to the food processor and mince again. Add the green chili, if using it, and the yogurt along with the salt and all the spices. Mince to a fine paste and transfer the contents to a bowl. Add the paneer and toss well to mix. Cover and marinate for 1 hour. When ready to grill, thread the paneer onto skewers and grill, covered, over medium heat until lightly browned, about 10 minutes. Turn occasionally and baste with the leftover marinade. At the end of cooking time, uncover the grill, turn up the heat slightly, and char the paneer for 2 minutes more. Slide the paneer off the skewers, heap onto a platter, and serve sprinkled liberally with lemon juice.

Chili Paneer

Cottage cheese marinated in green chilies ginger, garlic,
fresh coriander, and soy sauce

Indians have always borrowed freely from cuisines brought to them by invading armies or trading fleets. One of the lesser-known sources of inspiration has been China. There is a well-established Chinese community in India, concentrated mainly in Calcutta, which was once the center of a booming trade with Shanghai. Chinese restaurants have become increasingly popular all over India and, adapting to local tastes, have developed a unique repertoire that incorporates Indian ingredients and spices in Chinese recipes. Chili Paneer is a good example of the merging of Indian and Chinese cooking styles. It lives up to its name—the green chilies and black pepper are very hot—so to temper the heat, you could omit the black pepper and deseed the green chilies. Chili Paneer makes a great appetizer, or you could team it up with Aadoo Murgh (chicken grilled with fresh peaches, page 70) or Moghlai Tikka (chicken and pineapple marinated in almonds, cashew nuts, coconut, and cream, page 63).

½-inch piece of ginger, peeled

4 cloves of garlic, peeled

4 hot green chilies

1 cup loosely packed fresh coriander leaves, washed and drained

Salt to taste

½ teaspoon black pepper

2 tablespoons white vinegar

2 tablespoons soy sauce

2 tablespoons sesame oil

2 tablespoons tomato ketchup

1 teaspoon sugar

½ lb. paneer (cottage cheese), diced into ½-inch cubes

15–20 shiitake mushrooms, stemmed

1 sweet red pepper, deseeded and diced into 1-inch pieces

Lemon juice

SERVES 4

In a food processor, finely mince the ginger, garlic, and green chilies. Add the coriander, salt, pepper, vinegar, soy sauce, sesame oil, ketchup, and sugar and mince again. Transfer to a bowl, then mix in the cubes of paneer. Cover and marinate for no longer than 1 hour, as the cheese tends to get a little chewy otherwise. Toss the mushrooms and red pepper into the marinade along with the paneer. Skewer the paneer and the vegetables, alternating a cube of paneer between each vegetable. Grill, covered, on medium heat, basting occasionally with the leftover marinade until evenly browned, about 10 minutes. Uncover the grill, turn up the heat slightly, and char the paneer for 2 minutes more. Serve with a dash of lemon juice.

NOTE: If you have leftover marinade, it can be used as a sauce for the cheese and vegetables. You can also thicken the sauce with some cornstarch.

kaju methi paneer ke tikke

*Grilled cottage cheese and green peppers marinated
and served in a sauce of cashew nuts, dried fenugreek
leaves, tomatoes, and cream*

Ready-made *paneer* (cottage cheese) is available in all Indian
stores and is becoming a familiar sight at other grocery stores. If, however, you
find it hard to obtain, or would prefer to make your own, it is quite easy to do.
Living in a small New York town with no Indian grocery store in sight, I got a
lot of practice making my own paneer. I made it in bulk and froze extra batches
for later use. I have described how to make paneer in "Getting Prepared," page
xxvi.

2 tablespoons
vegetable oil

½ teaspoon cumin
seeds

½ -inch piece of
ginger, peeled
and minced

2 cloves of garlic,
peeled and
minced

¼ cup unroasted,
unsalted cashew
nuts, powdered

1 cup diced
tomatoes, fresh
or canned

½ teaspoon
turmeric

¼ teaspoon cayenne
pepper

½ teaspoon garam
masala

½ teaspoon ground
coriander seeds

¼ teaspoon ground
cumin seeds

2 teaspoons dried
fenugreek leaves

Salt to taste

½ lb. paneer
(cottage cheese),
diced into 1-inch
cubes

1 medium green
bell pepper,
stemmed,
deseeded, and
cut into 1-inch
cubes

2 tablespoons
heavy cream

Lemon juice

SERVES 4

In a skillet, heat the oil over a
medium-high flame and add the
cumin seeds. After a few seconds, add
the minced ginger and garlic. Sauté
for 1 minute, then add the powdered
cashew nuts. Sauté, stirring for 1
minute, then add the diced tomatoes.
Stir well to mix, mashing the tomatoes with the back of your spoon to
soften them. Add all the spices and
salt and mix well. Cook for 5 to 8
minutes, or until the tomatoes have
softened and blended into the sauce.
Cool to room temperature, then
transfer the sauce to a serving bowl
and toss in the cubes of paneer.

Marinate, covered at room temperature, for 1 hour. When ready to grill, lift the paneer out of its marinade, shaking out and reserving the excess marinade as you do so, and thread onto skewers, alternating with the diced green pepper. Grill, covered, over medium heat for about 10 minutes. Uncover the grill, turn up the heat slightly, and char the paneer for 2 minutes more. To serve, remove the paneer and green pepper from the skewers and toss them back into the remaining marinade in the mixing bowl. Mix in the heavy cream and add the lemon juice to taste.

Paneer durbari

*Grilled cottage cheese served in a tomato cream sauce
with sautéed onion and green pepper*

Cheese making, which has been raised to such a fine art in Europe, never really developed in India. Most Indians are vegetarians and will not eat rennet, which is used in cheese preparation. *Paneer* (cottage cheese), which is the only form of cheese that originated in India, is made using either lemon juice or yogurt to curdle the milk. To compensate for having only one kind of cheese, Indian cooks devise countless ways to serve paneer, often combining it with vegetables for variety.

For the marinade:

- 4 cloves of garlic, peeled
- 1 -inch piece of ginger, peeled
- 4 tablespoons lemon juice
- Salt to taste
- ½ teaspoon ground black pepper
- ¼ teaspoon red cayenne pepper (optional)
- ½ teaspoon cumin seeds
- ½ lb. paneer (cottage cheese), diced into ½-inch pieces

For the sauce:

- 1 cup diced tomatoes, fresh or canned
- 1 tablespoon vegetable oil
- 1 tablespoon butter

- ½ teaspoon cumin seeds
- 1 medium onion, peeled and chopped into ½-inch pieces
- 1 medium sweet green pepper, deseeded and diced into ½-inch pieces
- Salt to taste
- ½ teaspoon ground black pepper
- 1 teaspoon sugar
- ½ teaspoon turmeric
- ½ teaspoon ground coriander seeds
- 1 tablespoon dried fenugreek leaves, optional
- 1 teaspoon garam masala
- 3 tablespoons heavy cream

SERVES 4

In a food processor, blend all marinade ingredients, except the cumin seeds, to a smooth paste, scraping down the sides of the bowl with a spatula. Transfer the contents of the processor to a mixing bowl and add the cumin seeds and the diced paneer. Marinate for 1 hour. Meanwhile, prepare the sauce. Whirl the diced tomatoes to a purée in a blender or food processor. Heat the oil and butter over a medium-high flame. Add the cumin seeds and, after a few seconds, the diced onion and green pepper. Sauté for about 3 to 4 minutes, then add the tomato purée and all the remaining ingredients except the heavy cream. Cook, stirring for about 7 to 8 minutes, then remove from heat and stir in the heavy cream. Set aside. Thread the cubes of paneer onto skewers and spread any leftover marinade over them. Grill, covered, on medium heat until lightly browned, turning the skewers carefully for evenness, about 10 minutes. Uncover the grill, turn up the heat slightly, and char the paneer lightly for 2 minutes more. When all the skewers are done, slide the paneer off them and put the pieces in the sauce. Warm gently over medium heat, stirring occasionally for about 2 minutes. If the sauce seems too thick, you may add $\frac{1}{4}$ cup or more of water to achieve the desired consistency. Transfer to a bowl and serve.

bhune alu masaledaar

Crispy potatoes marinated in spices, fresh coriander, and olive oil

Potatoes are cooked in so many different ways in India that entire cookbooks could be devoted to them. I was amazed to learn that potatoes were introduced relatively recently to India; the Portuguese probably brought them from South America in the seventeenth century. I still don't know how Indians managed to cook before that! This versatile recipe can be served as a side dish, as a warm potato salad tossed with green onions and fresh coriander, or in Dhaniye aur Dahi ka Masala (yogurt sauce with fresh coriander and ginger, page 170) for a substantial entrée. A salad goes especially well with it.

2 lb. small new potatoes, washed

1 medium onion, peeled

4 cloves of garlic, peeled

1 -inch piece of ginger, peeled

1 cup tightly packed fresh coriander leaves and tender upper stems, washed and drained

1 green chili, optional

Salt to taste

¼–½ teaspoon ground black pepper

1 teaspoon garam masala

1 teaspoon ground coriander seeds

1 teaspoon ground cumin seeds

¼ cup lemon juice

¼ cup olive oil or vegetable oil

SERVES 4

Put the potatoes in a microwave-safe bowl and cover them with water; seal with plastic wrap and microwave on high for 10 minutes. The potatoes should be almost cooked but not too soft. Drain and halve the larger potatoes. Set aside. In a food processor, mince the onion, garlic, ginger, fresh coriander, and green chili. Mince well. Scrape down the sides with a spatula and add the salt, pepper, garam masala, ground coriander, ground cumin, lemon juice, and oil. Mix well and transfer to a large bowl. With a toothpick, pierce each potato a few times and toss them into the marinade. Cover the bowl and marinate for at least 1 hour. When ready to grill, thread the potatoes onto skewers and grill, covered, over medium heat until crisp and brown on the outside and cooked through on the inside, about 10 minutes. Baste occasionally with the leftover marinade. Uncover the grill, turn up the heat slightly, and lightly char the potatoes for a few minutes more. To serve, slide the potatoes off the skewers and heap them on a platter.

Tandoori Gobhi

Cauliflower florets marinated in yogurt and spices

Cauliflower is ideally suited to grilling—no other cooking method is capable of eliciting such an irresistible aroma from it. I find that cooking the cauliflower slightly before putting it on the barbecue helps it cook faster and also prevents it from drying out during grilling. Adding chickpea flour to the marinade makes the cauliflower crisp and golden when it comes off the grill. If you don't have any, substitute bread crumbs to achieve a similar effect.

1½ lb. cauliflower (about 1 medium head), cut into ¾-inch florets

4 tablespoons chickpea flour (besan)

2 cups plain yogurt (not low-fat)

1 -inch piece of ginger, peeled and grated or minced

4 cloves of garlic, peeled and grated or minced

Salt to taste

¼–½ teaspoon cayenne pepper

¾ teaspoon garam masala

½ teaspoon ground cumin seeds

¾ teaspoon ground coriander seeds

½ cup loosely packed fresh coriander leaves, chopped

Vegetable oil for basting

Lemon juice

SERVES 4

Fill a pot with enough water to cover the cauliflower florets and bring to a rolling boil. Add the florets and simmer, uncovered, for 5 minutes. Drain and set aside. In a big mixing bowl, combine the chickpea flour and yogurt, mixing with a spoon until smooth. Add the ginger and garlic, the salt, all the dry spices, and the fresh coriander leaves. Mix, then add the cauliflower florets and toss well in the marinade. At this point, you can either grill them right away or let them marinate for up to 24 hours until you are ready to cook.

Thread the cauliflower onto skewers, baste with marinade, and grill, covered, on medium heat until lightly browned and cooked through, about 10 minutes. During the last 5 minutes of cooking time, baste with the vegetable oil and uncover the grill to lightly char them. When cool enough to handle, slide them off the skewers, heap onto a platter, and sprinkle with lemon juice.

bhuna hua bhurta

Roasted eggplant, onions, and tomatoes sautéed with spices

Preparations for making bhurta in village kitchens usually start a day in advance when an eggplant is placed in the dying embers of the wood-stove to char in the fading heat. City dwellers who cook on gas stoves lament the loss of the charred aroma that characterizes true bhurta. Cooking it on a barbecue is one way to achieve the authentic flavor of this dish. I even like to barbecue the onions and tomatoes that go into the making of bhurta because I find that the flavor intensifies. I usually roast the vegetables at the end of a barbecue cookout and then make bhurta the next day. Bhurta goes well with all Indian breads.

1 medium
  eggplant (1 lb.)

1 large tomato
  (½ lb.)

1 medium onion,
  peeled

2 cloves of garlic,
  peeled

2 tablespoons
  vegetable oil

½ teaspoon cumin
  seeds

½ teaspoon ground
  coriander seeds

½ teaspoon ground
  cumin seeds

¼ teaspoon garam
  masala

¼ teaspoon cayenne
  pepper

  Salt to taste

1 tablespoon
  chopped fresh
  coriander leaves
  (optional)

SERVES 4

Pierce the eggplant a few times with a skewer or a toothpick and grill, covered, over low heat for about 20 to 25 minutes, turning occasionally. The eggplant should be completely cooked through and smell roasted by the end of the cooking time. Wrap the tomato, onion, and garlic individually in foil and grill alongside the eggplant. The garlic should be done in about 8 to 10 minutes, the tomato in about 20 minutes, and the onion in about 20 to 25 minutes. All the vegetables should smell roasted and be cooked through; remove the vegetables from the grill as they are done. Allow the vegetables to cool to room temperature, then cut off the stem end from the eggplant and remove the peel. Place the pulp in a bowl and mash it well with a fork. Chop the onion and garlic as finely as you can. Remove the tomato from the foil, saving all accumulated juices from the foil cup. Peel the tomato and mash it well with a fork. Heat the oil over a medium-high flame and put in the cumin seeds. After a few seconds, add the chopped onions and garlic. Sauté for about 2 to 3 minutes, until lightly browned. Add the mashed tomato and all the accumulated juices. Turn the heat to medium low and cook for about 3 to 4 minutes, or until the liquid has evaporated a little bit. Add all the spices and salt and cook for a minute. Stir in the mashed eggplant, mixing well. Cook for another 10 minutes, stirring occasionally. Mix in the fresh coriander leaves. Serve hot.

baingan kashmiri

Baby eggplant coated in a sweet-and-sour tamarind-fennel sauce served with grilled apples

Apples grow abundantly in the mountains of Kashmir; they cannot withstand the heat of the plains. The combination of apples with meat or vegetables, unusual elsewhere in India, is uniquely Kashmiri. The sweet-and-sour tamarind-fennel sauce, which coats the grilled eggplant, is a perfect foil for the tartness of the apple. Baingan Kashmiri goes well with Gosht Roghan Josh (lamb marinated in yogurt, almonds, and ground fennel seeds, page 94) or Kashmiri Murgh Elaichi (chicken breast marinated with yogurt, cardamom, and fennel, page 64).

A lime-sized ball of seedless tamarind (4 oz.), soaked in ½ cup hot water for at least 1 hour

1 tablespoon vegetable oil

½ -inch piece of ginger, peeled and grated

1 hot green chili, chopped finely

½ teaspoon cumin seeds

½ teaspoon turmeric

½ teaspoon ground coriander seeds

1 teaspoon fennel seeds, ground

2 teaspoons sugar

Salt to taste

5 long purple eggplant (about 1¼ lb.), washed, dried, and halved, intact at the stem

1 Granny Smith apple, peeled, halved, and cored

SERVES 4

Set a sieve over a bowl and squeeze the soaked tamarind through, discarding the fibrous residue. Heat the oil over a medium flame and add the grated ginger and chopped chili. Sauté for 1 minute, then add the cumin seeds. After a few seconds, add all the remaining spices, sugar, and salt. Stir for a few seconds, then add the tamarind extract. Cook for 2 minutes, then switch off the heat but let the pan remain on the stove to cool and thicken. When the sauce is cool enough to handle, stuff it in the eggplant. Wrap each eggplant in enough foil to make a snug packet. Grill the eggplant and the apple, covered, over medium heat until the apple is lightly charred but still slightly crisp, about 10 minutes. The eggplant should take about 15 minutes to be cooked through. Remove the eggplant from the foil and place on a platter. Thinly slice the apple and arrange around the eggplant.

alu moongphali aur paneer ke kabob

Croquettes of mashed potatoes, cottage cheese, and roasted peanuts

When I invite friends over for a barbecue, I always serve some form of seekh kabobs because they cook quickly and I can pass them around as appetizers while preparing the rest of the food. Guests cluster around the barbecue and help themselves to skewers as soon as they come off the grill. Vegetarians felt somewhat left out of this gathering, so I devised Alu Moongphali aur Paneer ke Kabob to have something on hand for them, and was pleased to find that they are equally popular with all my guests.

4 medium potatoes

½ cup roasted peanuts, powdered coarsely

1 small red onion, peeled and finely chopped

1 hot green chili, finely chopped (optional)

½ cup grated or crumbled paneer (cottage cheese)

2 tablespoons chopped fresh coriander leaves

½ teaspoon cumin seeds

Salt to taste

3 slices of white bread

Vegetable oil for basting

Lemon juice

SERVES 4

Boil the potatoes until tender. Cool and peel them. Mash them well with a fork and set aside. Mix the peanuts, the chopped onion and chili, the paneer, fresh coriander leaves, cumin seeds, and salt with the mashed potatoes. Wet the slices of bread under running water and squeeze out all the excess moisture. Mash them into the

potato mixture. Wetting your hands lightly whenever necessary, take a lemon-sized lump of the potato mixture in your hands and shape it into a croquette, flattening slightly. Proceed similarly with the remaining mixture. Place all the croquettes on an open barbecue on medium-high heat. Basting with the oil whenever necessary, grill the croquettes until lightly browned and slightly crisp on both sides, about 15 minutes. Serve with a squeeze of lemon juice.

bhutte ke kabob

Skewers of mashed potatoes and corn

Late summer, when fresh corn is in season, is the ideal time to make these kabobs. Use peaches-and-cream corn for best results. The easiest way to get the kernels off the cob is to wash the shucked corn, cover it tightly with plastic wrap, and microwave each cob for 3 minutes. When the cobs are cool enough to handle, the kernels can be cut off with ease. Coriander mint chutney makes a great dip for these kabobs.

4 medium potatoes (about 1 lb.)

1½ cups whole corn kernels (fresh or frozen), cooked and drained

½ -inch piece of ginger

Salt to taste

½ teaspoon ground black pepper

¼ teaspoon roasted ground cumin seeds

¼ teaspoon garam masala

Vegetable oil for basting

Lemon juice

SERVES 4

Boil the potatoes, cool and peel them. Mash them well with a fork and set aside. Combine the cooked corn kernels and the ginger in a food processor and mince. Add these to the mashed potatoes along with the salt, pepper, roasted ground cumin, and garam masala. Wetting your hands lightly whenever necessary, take a lemon-sized ball of the mixture in your hands and mold it onto skewers in 4- to 6-inch-long sausage shapes, pressing gently with your fingertips to keep the kabob in place. Grill, uncovered, on medium heat until golden brown all over, about 15 minutes. Baste with the vegetable oil now and then and turn occasionally to ensure even cooking. Serve with a sprinkle of lemon juice.

Chane ki tikki

Croquettes of mashed chickpeas, potatoes, and spices

Dried peas, legumes, and beans are an excellent source of protein for vegetarians. Indians eat them at almost every meal and have created many recipes for their use. Here, chickpeas are mashed with potatoes and formed into croquettes, which are then grilled. Bread replaces egg as a binder to hold the croquettes together, thus making it completely vegetarian. You can serve them on rolls, like burgers, with sliced tomatoes and lettuce.

1 medium potato

1 medium onion, peeled and coarsely chopped

2 cloves of garlic, peeled and coarsely chopped

½ -inch piece of ginger, peeled and coarsely chopped

2 green chilies (optional), peeled and coarsely chopped

2 cups cooked chickpeas, fresh or canned, washed and drained

Salt to taste

¼–½ teaspoon cayenne pepper

½ teaspoon garam masala

½ teaspoon roasted ground cumin seeds

2 tablespoons chopped fresh coriander leaves

2 slices of white bread

Vegetable oil for basting

Lemon juice

SERVES 4

Boil the potato until tender, cool and peel it. Set aside. In a food processor, mince the onion, garlic, ginger, and green chilies, if using, then add the chickpeas and mince again. Chop the potato and add it to the processor along with the salt, cayenne, garam masala, and roasted cumin. Whirl until everything is well blended, then transfer the contents to a mixing bowl and add the fresh coriander leaves. Dip the bread in a bowl of water and squeeze it with your hands to get rid of all the moisture. Add the bread to the potatoes in the mixing bowl and mix well with a fork or with your hands. Divide the mixture into eight equal balls and flatten them lightly with your hands. Brush them lightly all over with the vegetable oil and grill, uncovered, over medium-high heat until lightly browned, turning once. This should take about 15 minutes. Serve hot with a squeeze of lemon juice.

alu matar ki tikki

Croquettes of mashed potatoes stuffed with green peas, ginger, and spices

One of my favorite treats when growing up in Delhi was going shopping with my mother. We would board a bus to Janpath, a street that has the most exciting shops and also offers the best *chaat*. Chaat are various savory snacks, typically sold from pushcarts by roadside vendors. Some of the food is already prepared and only needs to be tossed together with spicy or sweet-and-sour chutneys and topped with chopped onions, tomatoes, and fresh coriander. One of our favorites, Alu Tikkis, were shallow-fried right in front of us on a little charcoal stove and served with yogurt and a sweet-and-sour tamarind chutney. Here, I have grilled the tikkis instead of shallow frying them; the taste is just as good as I remember. You can serve them with Hare Aam ki Chatni (roasted green mango chutney with fresh herbs, green chilies, and roasted garlic, page 48) and some yogurt.

4 medium potatoes (about 1 lb.)

3 slices of white bread

Salt to taste

1 cup frozen green peas

1 hot green chili, finely chopped (optional)

¼ -inch piece of ginger, finely chopped

1 tablespoon chopped fresh coriander leaves

¼ teaspoon garam masala

¼ teaspoon roasted ground cumin seeds

Vegetable oil for basting

Lemon juice

SERVES 4

Boil the potatoes until tender. Cool, peel, and mash them well with a fork. Wet the slices of bread under running water and thoroughly squeeze out the moisture. Mix the mashed bread and salt into the potatoes. Set aside. Cook the peas until tender. Drain and mash them well with a fork. Add the green chili and ginger to the mashed peas along with salt to taste, fresh coriander, garam masala, and cumin. Mix well and set aside. Wetting your hands lightly when necessary, form an equal number of balls with the potato mixture. You should have about 12 lime-sized balls when you are done. Flatten each ball slightly and put 1 to 2 tablespoons of the mashed pea stuffing in the center of half of the balls. Cover with the remaining flattened balls and seal the edges by lightly pressing together. Place on an open grill on medium-high heat, brushing the vegetable oil once lightly on each side and flipping the croquettes now and then for even cooking. Grill until the croquettes are lightly golden and crisp on the outside, about 15 minutes. Serve with a dash of lemon juice or with a chutney of your choice.

alu bhari simla mirch

Green peppers stuffed with spicy sautéed potatoes

When my mother invites friends for a meal, they often request her justly famous stuffed green peppers, which are shallow-fried with a bit of oil. Grilling them, however, allows the unique aroma of roasted green peppers to permeate the stuffing, making the dish fragrant and delicious. It also cuts down on the amount of oil used in its preparation. For an all-vegetarian meal, you could serve these peppers with Kaju Methi Paneer ke Tikke (grilled cottage cheese and green peppers in a sauce of cashew nuts, fenugreek leaves, tomatoes, and cream, page 128) or with Bhuna Baingan Masalewala (eggplant slices grilled with spiced oil). They also go well with Machali Masala (grilled breaded salmon steaks, page 104).

4 small sweet green peppers, washed, dried, and stemmed (reserve stems)

Salt to taste

3 medium potatoes

2 tablespoons vegetable oil

½ teaspoon cumin seeds

½ teaspoon turmeric

¼–½ teaspoon cayenne pepper

½ teaspoon ground coriander seeds

½ teaspoon garam masala

1 tablespoon lemon juice

SERVES 4

Lightly salt the insides of the green peppers and set aside. Boil the potatoes, cool and peel them, and finely chop them. In a skillet, heat the oil over a medium flame and add the cumin seeds. After a few seconds, add the turmeric, cayenne pepper, and ground coriander seeds. Stir quickly for a few seconds, then put in the potatoes and salt to taste. Mix well and sauté for 2 to 3 minutes. Remove from heat, cool to room temperature, and mix in the garam masala and lemon juice. Stuff the potato mixture into the green peppers, leaving a slight depression in the center for the caps to fit. When all the peppers have been stuffed, put the reserved stem caps on firmly. Grill the peppers, covered, on medium heat for about 15 minutes, turning them around occasionally so they char lightly but evenly. During the last few minutes of cooking time, uncover the grill, turn up the heat slightly, and lightly char the peppers. The peppers should be cooked through and softened.

NOTE: The potatoes can be made up to 2 days in advance if kept refrigerated.

kaddoo ki sabzi

Roasted pumpkin with onions and fenugreek seeds

Fresh pumpkins heaped on front porches at Halloween remind me of feasts in India, where pumpkin dishes hold the place of honor. One Halloween, my friend Karen Cormier proudly presented me with a beautiful pumpkin from her garden. Not seeing it displayed, she maintained a polite silence for a few days but finally couldn't help asking what had happened to it; she was horrified to discover that my family had eaten it! Most Indians would be equally aghast to learn that Halloween pumpkins are used as decorations rather than as food. The recipe given here, one from my mother-in-law's repertoire, is an everyday dish, which can be served with naan and Tandoori Murgh Kari (chicken marinated in sautéed onions, tomatoes, and spices, page 68).

1 lb. peeled and deseeded pumpkin, cut into 1-inch pieces

1½ cups water

For the marinade:

3 tablespoons vegetable oil

½ teaspoon garam masala

Salt to taste

For the sauce:

3 tablespoons vegetable oil

¼ teaspoon fenugreek seeds

2 medium onions, peeled and thinly sliced

2 cloves of garlic, peeled and thinly sliced

2 green chilies, deseeded if desired and finely chopped

1 tablespoon ground fennel seeds

¾ teaspoon ground coriander seeds

½ teaspoon ground cumin seeds

½ teaspoon turmeric

2 teaspoons sugar

1 tablespoon lemon juice

SERVES 4

Put the pumpkin, covered with water, in a microwave-safe bowl. Seal tightly with plastic wrap and microwave on high for 8 minutes, then drain and cool. In a mixing bowl, combine the vegetable oil, garam masala, and salt. Toss in the pumpkin and coat well with the spiced oil. Skewer the pieces and grill on an open fire on medium-high heat for about 10 minutes. The pumpkin should be soft and charred in spots all over. Slide the pieces off the skewers and put back into the marinating bowl. Warm the remaining oil over medium-high heat and add the fenugreek seeds. After a few seconds, add the sliced onions, garlic, and green chilies and sauté for about 8 to 10 minutes, or until golden brown. Add all the remaining ingredients except the lemon juice. Sauté, stirring, for 2 minutes, then put in the barbecued pumpkin. Coat the pieces gently with the spices and cook, covered, on low heat for 5 minutes, being careful not to mash the pieces. Mix in the lemon juice and additional garam masala if necessary.

bharvan guchchi

*Portobello mushrooms marinated in vinegar and spices,
stuffed with spiced feta cheese*

The ingredients in this dish may not seem very Indian; this recipe is my contribution to fusion cuisine. I was inspired to try my hand at it after reading a newspaper article on blending Indian food with other cuisines. I discovered that Portobello mushrooms and feta cheese lend themselves exceptionally well to Indian spices and flavorings. Marinating the mushrooms before stuffing them allows them to soak up all the flavor of the marinade. Bharvan Guchchi also makes a good appetizer.

10 medium Portobello mushrooms (1 lb.), washed, dried, and stemmed (finely chop and reserve stems)

For the filling:

1 tablespoon vegetable oil

1 bay leaf

¼ teaspoon cumin seeds

1 small onion, finely chopped

1 hot green chili (optional), finely chopped

2 tablespoons chopped fresh coriander leaves

¼ cup bread crumbs

Salt to taste

¼ teaspoon ground black pepper

¼ cup crumbled feta cheese

For the marinade:

2 tablespoons vinegar

1 tablespoon lemon juice

1 teaspoon sugar

Salt to taste

2 tablespoons chopped fresh coriander leaves

1 clove of garlic, grated

½ teaspoon garam masala

1 tablespoon olive oil

SERVES 4

In a skillet, heat oil over a medium flame and add the bay leaf and cumin seeds. After a few seconds, add the chopped onion and chili. Sauté for about 5 minutes, then put in the chopped mushroom stems. Sauté for another 2 minutes, then remove the pan from the heat. Mix in all the remaining ingredients for the filling and set aside. Mix together all the marinade ingredients in a bowl and toss in the mushroom caps. Spoon the marinade all over them and marinate for 1 hour. When ready to grill, lift the caps out of their marinade and arrange them in a plate. Stuff them with the feta cheese mixture, pressing down gently to keep the filling in place. Grill the mushrooms, stuffed side up, on an open barbecue over medium heat for about 10 minutes. Do not flip them over. Lift them off the barbecue and arrange on a platter.

guchchi ki sabzi

Grilled mushrooms served in a sauce of sautéed onion, tomatoes, and cream

A century ago the only people in India who ate mushrooms were the British, who imported them from England in cans. Even a few decades ago it was difficult to obtain fresh mushrooms in most parts of the country, and they were rarely used in Indian cooking. However, in recent years mushrooms have become very popular and something of a status symbol in India. It is a rare wedding banquet where you will not see them served. I once had button mushrooms in a mildly spiced, creamy sauce and thought it a great dish. After adapting it to the barbecue, I found that the grilled aroma of the mushrooms added wonderfully to the flavor of Guchchi ki Sabzi, making it a perennial favorite with my son Rohan. The taste of this dish improves if you cook it a day in advance of serving it. Rice is a good accompaniment.

For the marinade:

Salt to taste

¼ teaspoon ground black pepper

¼ cup vegetable oil

1 lb. small white mushrooms, washed and drained

For the sauce:

1 medium onion, peeled and coarsely chopped

2 cloves of garlic, peeled and coarsely chopped

1 cup diced tomatoes, canned or fresh

2 tablespoons vegetable oil

½ teaspoon cumin seeds

1½ cups water

Salt to taste

½ teaspoon turmeric

½ teaspoon garam masala

½ teaspoon ground coriander seeds

¼ cup heavy cream

SERVES 4

Mix the salt, pepper, and vegetable oil together in a bowl and toss in the mushrooms. Coat well and marinate for 15 minutes at room temperature, tossing once in a while. When ready to grill, lift the mushrooms out of the marinade and thread onto skewers. Grill, covered, on a medium-hot barbecue for about 8 to 10 minutes, flipping the skewers for even grilling. When the mushrooms are lightly browned and cooked (you can slice one to see if it is moist inside and not raw), slide them off the skewers and into a bowl. Cover and set aside.

To prepare the sauce, put the onion, garlic, and tomatoes in a blender or food processor and blend to a fairly smooth purée. Heat the oil over a medium-high flame and add the cumin seeds. After 1 minute, add the puréed onions from the blender. Sauté for about 15 minutes, stirring frequently. When all the liquid has evaporated and the raw smell dissipates, it is done. Add the water, salt, and all the spices. Increase heat and bring the contents of the pan to a boil. Reduce heat to low, cover, and cook for about 10 minutes, stirring now and then. Remove the pan from the heat and mix in the heavy cream and the grilled mushrooms. Let the pan sit for 5 minutes, allowing for the flavors to mingle before serving.

NOTE: This dish can be made up to 2 days in advance. When reheating it, make sure not to bring it to a boil; just warm it gently over medium heat.

RICE

Subz biryani *Grilled mixed vegetables cooked with rice, coconut milk, and spices*

Tamatar ka Pulao *Rice cooked with peas in a roasted tomato purée* **Guchchi wala Pulao** *Rice cooked with grilled mushrooms and sweet red peppers* **Kashmiri Murgh Chaval** *Rice cooked with grilled chicken and garam masala*

Murgh biryani *Rice cooked with grilled chicken curry* **Gosht biryani** *Rice cooked with spicy grilled lamb curry* **Masala Makhan** *Spicy garlic butter*

*I*f you dine in *dhabas*, the small roadside eateries that are a familiar sight in India, you will find that there is no charge for the vegetables or lentils; you will be billed only for the *naan* or *roti* (flatbreads cooked in a tandoor). This practice captures an essential difference between Indian and Western concepts of food—a western meal is planned around a meat entrée complemented by other dishes, while rice or bread lies at the heart of an Indian meal. When planning a meal, you must first decide whether you will serve a rice dish or pick from one of the many kinds of bread. This choice then guides the selection of the remaining menu. All dishes are classified as "wet," which incorporate a sauce to be poured over rice, or "dry," which can be scooped up with bread.

Indian cuisine boasts a large variety of breads: *chapatis*, made from unleavened whole wheat dough; deep fried puffy *puris*; shallow-fried *parathas* stuffed with meat or vegetables; and deep fried *kachoris* filled with spicy lentils. Two types of bread cooked in the tandoor are *naan*, made from leavened white flour, and *tandoori roti*, made from unleavened whole wheat dough. To make these, balls of dough are flattened out and slapped onto the hot walls of the tandoor where they stick and cook quickly. If making naan sounds intimidating, all you have to do is visit your grocery store, where ready-made naan is easily available.

You can also plan your meal around rice, which can be an entire meal in itself. Rice dishes range from the humble *kitchree* (a simple dish of rice and lentils, which the British adopted as kedgeree) to the elegant *pulao* and royal *biryani*. The distinction between these last two is subtle: a biryani is a meat or chicken curry layered with rice, whereas a pulao is rice to which meat or vegetables have been added.

In this chapter, I present recipes for pulaos and biryanis made with grilled ingredients. Although I specify basmati rice for each recipe, you can substitute the long-grained variety if you wish.

subz biryani

Grilled mixed vegetables cooked with rice, coconut milk, and spices

My aunt Mithlesh, who makes an excellent biryani, contributes her recipe here. The only change I make is to grill the vegetables before adding them to the rice. Her secret to great taste is cooking the rice without any water, using only a mixture of milk and coconut milk. This dish was a favorite with everybody in her family and was always made whenever I visited them. My cousins and I would cluster in the kitchen, catching up on each other's news and sampling the contents of the biryani while it was being made. My aunt indulgently tried to work around us. Subz Biryani is a meal by itself and needs only Thayir Pachadi (cucumber with grilled potatoes, onions, and tomatoes in yogurt, page 43) to complete it.

For the vegetable curry:

1 fresh corn on the cob, shucked

1 sweet red pepper, halved, seeded, and stemmed

1 green bell pepper, halved, seeded, and stemmed

1 red onion, peeled and halved

½ medium green zucchini, halved lengthwise

½ medium yellow zucchini, halved lengthwise

1 carrot

2 tablespoons vegetable oil

8-10 curry leaves, preferably fresh

½ -inch piece of ginger, grated

2 cloves of garlic, grated

1 hot green chili, finely chopped

1 teaspoon cumin seeds, powdered

1 teaspoon fennel seeds, powdered

4 whole green cardamom, powdered

4 whole cloves, powdered

½ teaspoon whole black pepper, powdered

½ -inch stick of cinnamon, powdered

2 medium red tomatoes, finely chopped

For the rice:

½ cup frozen peas

Salt to taste

1 cup basmati rice, washed and drained

1 cup canned coconut milk

1 cup milk, 2% or whole

2 tablespoons chopped fresh coriander leaves

SERVES 4

Roast the corn, peppers, onion, zucchini, and carrot in a covered barbecue on medium heat, turning for evenness. When the vegetables are lightly charred (cooking times will vary for each vegetable), remove them from the grill and cool. Using a sharp knife, cut away the kernels from the corn cob. Cut the green and red pepper into small pieces. Finely chop the onion. Cut the carrot into small bits. Dice the zucchini into half-inch pieces.

In a skillet, heat the oil over a medium flame and put in the curry leaves. After a few seconds, add the chopped onion, ginger, garlic, and chili. Sauté for 2 minutes, then add all the chopped roasted vegetables. Sauté for another 2 minutes. Add the powdered spices and the chopped tomatoes to the vegetables in the pan and cook for 5 minutes, or until slightly softened. Set this vegetable curry aside.

In another pan, add the peas, salt, washed and drained rice, coconut milk, and 2% milk. Cover the pan and bring to a boil. Immediately reduce heat to low and cook the rice, covered, for 15 minutes. Preheat the oven to 250°F. In a large ovenproof dish, spread a layer of half the rice. Top it with a layer of half the vegetables from the curry, lifting the vegetables out of the sauce with a slotted spoon. Add another layer of rice and top it with the remaining vegetables. Drizzle the leftover vegetable sauce all over and spread the fresh coriander leaves on top. Cover the dish tightly with foil and bake for 20 minutes. Stir the biryani gently with a fork and serve.

Tamatar ka pulao

Rice cooked with peas in a roasted tomato purée

"Rice with miscellaneous" was the rather cryptic entry I saw on a Chinese restaurant menu. While I lacked the courage to order the dish, I do feel that the name is a pretty good description of a *pulao*. Pulao is mildly spiced rice cooked with assorted vegetables, meat, or chicken. Any number of ingredients can go into the making of pulaos—fried onions, peas, shredded carrots, mixed vegetables, or whatever you can find in your refrigerator. While pulaos are usually cooked in water, sometimes a purée of spinach, tomatoes, or coconut milk is used as a medium for cooking the rice, each adding its own flavor to the dish. In this recipe, I use a purée of grilled tomatoes, which imparts a mild roasted aroma to the rice.

3 medium ripe
tomatoes (about
1 lb.)

2 tablespoons
vegetable oil

½ teaspoon cumin
seeds

A small stick of
cinnamon

2 green cardamom

2 whole cloves

5–7 whole black
peppercorns

1 medium onion,
peeled, halved,
and thinly sliced

1 cup basmati rice,
washed, drained,
and soaked in 1
cup cold water

Salt to taste

½ teaspoon
turmeric

1 cup frozen peas

SERVES 4

Wrap the tomatoes individually in aluminum foil and grill, covered, on medium–low heat for about 20 minutes. They should be mushy and smell roasted when they are done. Let cool, then lift the tomatoes out of their foil wrappings, reserving any liquid left in the foil. Peel and mash them with a fork. Strain the pulp through a sieve if desired, adding all reserved liquid from the foil cups. Measure the tomato liquid; if you do not have a full cup, add enough water to make up the difference. In a skillet, heat the oil over medium heat, then add the cumin, cinnamon, cardamom, cloves, and peppercorns. As soon as the spices puff up and darken, add the sliced onion. Sauté for about 6 to 7 minutes, or until the onion is lightly browned. Add the tomato purée, the rice and its soaking water, salt, turmeric, and peas. Cover and bring to a rolling boil. Immediately reduce heat to very low and cook for 20 minutes without opening the lid. Let the rice sit for 5 minutes, then fluff it up with a fork and serve.

guchchi wala pulao

Rice cooked with grilled mushrooms and sweet red peppers

This is one of my favorite childhood recipes. As a child, I found its delicate flavor very soothing and always doused it liberally with *raita* (yogurt relish) for a very satisfying meal. My mother, who classified mushrooms as meat—which she didn't eat—would have nothing to do with cooking them. So my father and I would chop, sauté, sniff appreciatively, and savor the delicious mushroom dishes we cooked. You can serve this *pulao* (rice cooked with assortd vegetables, meat, or chicken) with any chicken or lamb dish of your choice.

Salt to taste

¼ teaspoon ground black pepper

¼ cup olive oil

1 lb. white mushrooms, washed and dried

1 medium sweet red pepper

2 tablespoons vegetable oil

½ teaspoon cumin seeds

2 whole cloves

2 green cardamom

½ -inch stick of cinnamon

10 whole black peppercorns

1 bay leaf

1 small onion, peeled and finely chopped

1 cup basmati rice, washed, drained, and soaked in 1½ cups cold water

SERVES 4

Add the salt and pepper to the olive oil and toss the mushrooms in it. Skewer the mushrooms and grill, covered, over medium heat for about 5 minutes on each side. When they are done, throw them back into the marinade. Roast the red pepper in a covered grill on medium heat until charred all over, about 15 minutes. Put the pepper in a paper bag to cool.

Lift the mushrooms out of any accumulated juices and thinly slice them. Peel and deseed the red pepper and cut it into half-inch cubes. Heat oil over a medium flame and put in the cumin seeds, cloves, cardamom, cinnamon, peppercorns, and bay leaf. As soon as the spices puff up and darken, add the onion. Sauté for 5 minutes until lightly browned. Now add the mushrooms, reserving the juices. Add the red pepper and sauté for 2 minutes. Add the rice and its soaking water, the reserved liquid from the mushrooms, and more salt to taste, and bring the whole thing to a boil. Immediately reduce heat to very low, cover, and cook for 20 minutes, or until all the water has been absorbed and the rice is done. Do not lift the lid while cooking. Let the rice sit for 5 minutes, then fluff it up with a fork and serve.

kashmiri murgh chaval

Rice cooked with grilled chicken and garam masala

Mealtime in a Kashmiri household is a family affair, with everyone seated on the floor eating from a communal platter. In the center is a mountain of rice from which people help themselves. Servings of meat, chicken, and vegetables are then poured over each portion and eaten with the utmost delicacy using just the fingertips. Indians relish eating rice with their fingers—it somehow tastes better that way. Eating with a fork and knife is considered akin to making love through an interpreter! To fully savor this dish, try eating it with your fingers, Kashmiri style, topped with Gosht Roghan Josh (lamb marinated in yogurt, almonds, and ground fennel seeds, page 94).

3 tablespoons vegetable oil

2 whole cardamom

2 whole cloves

½ -inch stick cinnamon

1 bay leaf

1 small onion, peeled and finely chopped

1 cup basmati or other long-grained rice, washed and soaked in 1½ cups chicken broth

Salt to taste

¾ teaspoon garam masala

½ lb. boneless, skinless chicken breast, washed and dried

SERVES 4

In a skillet, heat 2 tablespoons of the oil over a medium flame and add the cardamom, cloves, cinnamon, and bay leaf. As soon as they puff up and darken, add the chopped onion. Sauté for about 5 minutes, or until the onions are lightly browned. Add the rice, its soaking liquid, and the salt. Stir to mix, cover, and bring to a rolling boil. Immediately reduce the heat to very low and cook for about 20 minutes; do not lift the lid while cooking. Meanwhile, mix ¼ teaspoon of the garam masala with 1 tablespoon vegetable oil and rub it all over the chicken breast. Grill, covered, on medium heat until cooked through and lightly charred on both sides, about 10 minutes. Cool slightly, then cut the chicken into 1-inch pieces. When the rice has been cooking for 20 minutes, add the grilled chicken and ½ teaspoon garam masala. Switch off the heat, stir very gently to mix, and let the pan sit, covered, for 5 to 7 minutes more before serving.

murgh biryani

Rice cooked with grilled chicken curry

The flavor of any rice dish comes not only from the meat, vegetables, and spices that you add, but also from the rice you use. Indian cooks are very particular in specifying the kind of rice that they want for each dish. A true biryani is best made with basmati rice. Grown near the foothills of the Himalayas, this rice is cherished for its slender long grains, nutty flavor, and delicate aroma. When I cook basmati rice, not only my kitchen but my entire house becomes fragrant with its perfume. Murgh Biryani is an excellent way to use any kind of leftover grilled chicken.

For the sauce:

- 2 tablespoons vegetable oil

- ½ teaspoon cumin seeds

- 2 cloves of garlic, peeled and grated

- ½ -inch piece of ginger, peeled and grated

- 1 medium onion, peeled and finely chopped

- 2 medium tomatoes, chopped

- 2 tablespoons plain low-fat yogurt

- ½ cup water

- Salt to taste

- ½ teaspoon cayenne pepper

- ½ teaspoon ground coriander seeds

- ½ teaspoon ground cumin seeds

- ½ teaspoon garam masala

- 4 pieces of barbecued chicken, drumsticks and/or thighs (use from any recipe in this book), deboned and cut into bite-sized pieces

For the rice:

- 1 cup basmati rice, washed, drained, and soaked in 1 cup of water

- 2 whole cloves

- 2 whole cardamom

- Salt to taste

For the garnish (optional):

- 2 hard-boiled eggs

- ¼ cup cashew nuts, deep fried

- ½ cup mixed fresh coriander and mint leaves, chopped

To prepare the sauce, heat the oil in a skillet over a medium-high flame and add the cumin seeds. After a few seconds, put in the garlic, ginger, and onion. Sauté for about 5 minutes or until lightly browned. Add the tomatoes to the pan and cook for another 5 minutes, mashing the tomatoes well with the back of your spoon. Switch off the heat and stir in the yogurt and all the remaining ingredients for the sauce. Mix well, then add the grilled and deboned chicken.

Combine all the rice ingredients in a pan and bring to a boil. Immediately reduce heat to very low, cover, and cook for 12 minutes. Preheat the oven to 250°F. Put the rice in an ovenproof dish and pour the chicken curry over it. Seal tightly with foil and bake for 20 minutes. Uncover, fluff up the rice and chicken gently with a fork to mix them, and garnish with the optional ingredients if desired.

gosht biryani

Rice cooked with spicy grilled lamb curry

The centerpiece of any Moghlai banquet is always a biryani. Meat is first cooked in a spicy sauce, then layered with rice, sealed tightly, and slow-cooked over low heat. Just before serving, the biryani is gently mixed together and lavishly garnished with hard-boiled eggs, deep-fried almonds and raisins, and paper-thin silver leaf. Biryanis are traditionally cooked with lamb, though chicken, shrimp, and fish (including leftovers) make excellent substitutes. Grilling the meat before adding it to the sauce adds a new dimension to the dish.

For the marinade:

- 2 cloves of garlic, peeled and grated
- ½-inch piece of ginger, peeled and grated
- 4 tablespoons plain low-fat yogurt
- Salt to taste
- ½ teaspoon garam masala
- ½ lb. boneless lamb or beef, cut into 1-inch cubes

For the sauce:

- 2 tablespoons vegetable oil
- ½ teaspoon cumin seeds
- 1 medium onion, peeled and finely chopped
- 2 cloves of garlic, peeled and grated
- ½-inch piece of ginger, peeled and grated
- 1 medium tomato, chopped
- 2 tablespoons plain low-fat yogurt
- ½ teaspoon garam masala
- Salt to taste
- ½ teaspoon ground coriander seeds
- ½ teaspoon ground cumin seeds
- ½ cup water

For the rice:

- 1 cup basmati rice, washed well
- 1 cup milk
- Salt to taste
- 2 green cardamom
- 2 cloves
- 5–6 whole black peppercorns

Mix the garlic and ginger with the yogurt, salt, and garam masala. Toss in the meat, cover, and refrigerate overnight or for at least 4 hours. Thread the meat onto skewers and grill in a covered barbecue on medium heat until almost done, about 15 minutes. Remove the meat from skewers and set aside. In a skillet, warm the oil over medium-high heat and put in the cumin seeds. After a few seconds, add the onion, garlic, and ginger. Sauté for 5 minutes, or until the onions are lightly browned. Add the tomato and cook for 5 minutes, mashing it well and incorporating it into the sauce. Turn off the heat and, with the pan still on the stove, add all the remaining ingredients for the sauce. Mix well, then put in the grilled meat.

Combine the rice and all the remaining ingredients in a pan. Cover, bring to a boil, then immediately reduce heat to very low. Cook until the rice is almost done, about 12 minutes. Preheat the oven to 250°F. Put the rice in an ovenproof dish and pour the grilled meat curry over it. Seal tightly with foil and bake for 20 minutes. Fluff up the biryani gently with a fork and serve.

masala makhan

Spicy garlic butter

This versatile butter can be brushed onto naans and other Indian breads. You can lightly grill store-bought naans then brush them with garlic butter. Masala Makhan can be used to make garlic bread or as a medium in which to serve grilled shrimp or scallops.

1 clove of garlic, peeled and grated

4 tablespoons salted butter, melted

¼ teaspoon garam masala

¼ teaspoon ground roasted cumin seeds

¼ teaspoon ground black pepper

SERVES 4

Combine all ingredients and mix well with a spoon. Use a pastry brush to brush it onto grilled naan or grilled bread. Cover and refrigerate unused portions.

Sauces

Makhani Tamatar ka Masala *Tomato sauce with butter and cream*

Tamatar Methi ka Masala *Tomato sauce with fenugreek and cream*

Tamatar Kaju ka Masala *Tomato sauce with cashew nuts and sour cream*

Dhaniye aur Dahi ka Masala *Yogurt sauce with fresh coriander and ginger*

there is no exact equivalent for the word "sauce" in Hindi. The closest translation is *masala*, which means a blend of herbs and spices mixed with onions, tomatoes, or yogurt, which forms a sauce in which food is cooked. Rather confusingly, in Indian-English the sauce for a dish is known as gravy, whereas "sauce" means ketchup. These linguistic subtleties were brought home to me when I attended my first American Thanksgiving dinner. On being offered gravy, I poured it liberally over my turkey, wondering why they hadn't cooked the bird in it in the first place. It wasn't until I tasted some that I realized it wasn't turkey curry that I was eating!

In Indian cuisine, the sauce is what gives the dish real flavor. Sauces are usually a combination of sautéed onions, tomatoes, or yogurt and a blend of spices that is tailored to suit each recipe. A good sauce complements the main ingredient and enhances its flavor, but does not overpower it. In this chapter I present four basic sauces in which you can serve grilled food. You can make them ahead of time and keep them refrigerated for up to 2 weeks. When barbecuing, double the recipe and save the leftover grilled food. With one of these sauces, you can serve a whole new dish the next day. You can create your own sauces by following the methods described in this chapter and varying the ingredients. For example, you can substitute yogurt or sour cream for the tomatoes to obtain a new flavor. These sauces make the dish more elegant and are ideal for dinner parties.

makhani tamatar ka masala

Tomato sauce with butter and cream

Makhan means butter; *makhani* describes any dish cooked in a butter-based sauce. A good example is butter chicken, found on most Indian restaurant menus. Makhani Tamatar ka Masala is used extensively in tandoori cooking to serve up barbecued chicken and lamb, and can be used to transform virtually any leftover barbecued food into a gourmet's delight. In fact, my family is so fond of it that I always grill extra tandoori chicken to serve up this way the next day. Two cups of this sauce is enough for about 2 lb. (6 to 8 pieces) of chicken.

4 tablespoons butter

1 clove of garlic, peeled and minced

1 small shallot, peeled and minced

2 cups diced tomatoes, canned or fresh

Salt to taste

¼–½ teaspoon ground black pepper

½ teaspoon garam masala

⅓ cup heavy cream

SERVES 4

In a skillet, heat 2 tablespoons of butter over a medium flame and add the garlic and shallots. Sauté for about 3 to 4 minutes, or until lightly browned. Whirl the tomatoes in the food processor and add to the browned shallots. Add salt, pepper, and garam masala. Cook, stirring occasionally, for about 8 to 10 minutes until the sauce is quite thick. Stir in the remaining butter until well blended, then remove the pan from heat. The sauce is now ready. You can either refrigerate it for up to a week or add the grilled food right away.

After the food has been added, cook on low heat for 5 to 8 minutes for the flavors to mingle. Remove from the heat and cool slightly for a few minutes. Gently mix in the heavy cream. The cream is added at the end, after the pan has been removed from the heat, to prevent the sauce from curdling.

Tamatar methi ka masala

Tomato sauce with fenugreek and cream

The flavor of fenugreek blends well with tomatoes and cream. I suggest using this sauce for barbecued foods—such as Murgh Kasoori (skewers of ground chicken marinated with fried onion and dried fenugreek leaves, page 58), Hari Machali (fish steaks marinated in fresh coriander, dried fenugreek leaves, and spices, page 106), Methiwala Gosht (skewers of ground lamb flavored with dried fenugreek leaves and spices, page 86), or Gosht Lajawab (lamb marinated in onion, fenugreek, and spices, page 96)—that already have some fenugreek in their marinade. Add the garam masala just before serving to keep the aroma of the fenugreek leaves from overpowering it during cooking.

2 tablespoons
butter

1 clove garlic,
peeled and
grated or minced

2 cups diced
tomatoes, canned
or fresh, puréed

3 tablespoons dried
fenugreek leaves

Salt to taste

¼–½ teaspoon ground
black pepper

½ teaspoon garam
masala

⅓ cup heavy cream

SERVES 4

Heat the butter over a medium flame and add the garlic. Sauté for 1 minute, then add the tomatoes, fenugreek leaves, salt, and pepper. Cook for about 10 minutes over a medium-low flame until the sauce has thickened. The sauce is now ready to be refrigerated for up to a week.

When ready to add the food, warm the sauce over a medium flame and put in up to 2 pounds of barbecued food. Cook on low heat for 10 minutes. Remove from heat, cool for 5 minutes, then gently mix in the garam masala and heavy cream.

Tamatar kaju ka masala

Tomato sauce with cashew nuts and sour cream

Cashew nuts are considered a luxury in Indian cuisine and are usually reserved for special occasions such as festivals and wedding feasts. Using them in everyday cooking would be considered ostentatious. Nevertheless, this is a quick and easy sauce if you have some cashew nuts in your kitchen closet. If you don't, try substituting unroasted almonds. You can also serve Tamatar Kaju ka Masala in a bowl on the side for dunking, or you can ladle it over a dish. A good way to use leftover barbecued meat would be to lightly cook it in this sauce before serving.

2 tablespoons vegetable oil

½ teaspoon cumin seeds

½ -inch piece of ginger, grated or minced

2 cloves of garlic, grated or minced

¼ cup unroasted, unsalted cashew nuts, powdered

1 cup diced tomatoes, fresh or canned, puréed

Salt to taste

¼ teaspoon turmeric

¼ teaspoon cayenne pepper

2 tablespoons sour cream

½ teaspoon garam masala

SERVES 4

In a skillet, heat the oil over a medium flame and add the cumin seeds. After a few seconds add the ginger and garlic and sauté for a few seconds. Add the cashew nut powder and stir-fry for a few seconds. Quickly put in the tomato purée and mix in the salt, turmeric, and cayenne pepper. Stirring frequently, cook over medium-low heat for about 5 minutes, or until the mixture is slightly thickened. Turn off the heat but do not remove the pan from the stove. Add the sour cream and garam masala and stir gently to mix. The sauce should be fairly thick by now and ready to eat.

You can either refrigerate the sauce for up to a week or serve it right away with up to 2 pounds of barbecued food. After adding the grilled food to the sauce, warm it gently over medium heat and cook for 5 minutes to blend the flavors.

dhaniye aur dahi ka masala

Yogurt sauce with fresh coriander and ginger

The cooking of Uttar Pradesh is distinctive for its simplicity and sparing use of garlic and onions, which many orthodox Hindus refuse to eat. Indian mythology relates that when a platter of fruits and vegetables was placed in front of the gods, the garlic and onion fell off, making them unclean. In the absence of onions as a thickening agent, yogurt and tomatoes are used liberally in most recipes. This sauce is typical of Uttar Pradesh cuisine, and potatoes and other vegetables are often cooked in it. I find that it is also a good medium for serving barbecued foods or even as a dipping sauce. You can thin it with a little water if you like, but be careful not to cook it too much or it will lose its fresh herbal flavor. Potatoes taste especially good in Dhaniye aur Dahi ka Masala, as does grilled zucchini or any kind of lamb kabok or chicken *tikka* (meat marinated in spices and grilled).

1 cup packed fresh coriander leaves and tender upper stems, washed and drained

½ -inch piece of ginger, peeled

1 hot green chili

½ cup water

½ teaspoon ground coriander seeds

½ teaspoon ground cumin seeds

½ teaspoon garam masala

½ teaspoon turmeric

¼ teaspoon cayenne pepper

Salt to taste

3 teaspoons water

2 tablespoons vegetable oil

½ teaspoon cumin seeds

1 cup plain low-fat yogurt

SERVES 4

In a blender, purée the fresh coriander, ginger, green chili, and ½ cup of water to a smooth paste. Combine the ground spices, salt, and 3 teaspoons of water in a small bowl. In a skillet, heat the oil over a medium flame and add the cumin seeds. After a few seconds, add the spice paste from the small bowl, standing back as you do so because it will splatter. Stir quickly for a few seconds to mix, then remove the pan from the stove. Stir in the yogurt and put the pan back on the stove. Cook for 5 minutes, stirring constantly to prevent the yogurt from curdling. Turn off the heat but let the pan sit on the hot stove. Mix in the fresh coriander paste from the blender and let the sauce cool over the fading heat of the stove.

This sauce will keep for a week in the refrigerator. If you want to cook barbecued food in it, then add the food to the sauce and warm it gently, taking care not to let it come to a boil. Cook for 5 minutes, then switch off the heat and let the food sit for 5 minutes before serving to let the flavors mingle.

index

a

Aadoo murgh, 70
Aam ki launji, 49
Achari kabobs, 91-92
Ajwain, xix
Alu bhari simla mirch,
  143-144
Alu ka raita, 42
Alu matar ki tikki, 141-142
Alu moongphali aur paneer
  ke kabob, 137-138
Angithi, xiv
Appetizers and Drinks,
  3-15
  Chicken breast marinated
    in a paste of sweet red
    peppers, onion, and
    spices, 11
  Chicken breast marinated
    in fresh coriander, gin-
    ger, and lemon juice, 10
  Crispy shrimp marinated
    with chickpea flour,
    eggs, and sour cream,
    12-13
  Grilled mushrooms
    marinated with spices,
    lemon juice, and fresh
    coriander, 6
  Grilled pappadums, 9
  Juice of roasted tomatoes
    with cumin and
    Tabasco, 13
  Mixed vegetables
    marinated in spicy oil
    and lemon juice, 8-9
  Roasted buttered corn
    with salt and lemon
    juice, 7
  Roasted garlic in spicy
    yogurt, 15
  Roasted green mango
    juice
Appliances and tools,
  necessary
  Electric coffee grinder,
    xxv
  Food processor
    or blender, xxv
  Skewers, xxv

b

Babar, xii, xiii
Baby eggplant coated in
  a sweet-and-sour
  tamarind-fennel sauce
  served with grilled
  apples, 136-137
Badaami seekh kabobs,
  87-88
Baingan ka raita, 39
Baingan kashmiri, 136-137
Basmati chaval, xxii
Basmati rice, xxii
Besan, xxii
Bharvan guchchi, 147-148
Bharvan murgh, 80-81
Bhuna baingan masal
  ewala, 124
Bhuna hua bhurta, 134-135
Bhuna hua bhutta, 7
Bhuna murga saagwala, 71

Bhune alu masaledaar,
  132-133
Bhune hue papad, 9
Bhune tamatar aur pyaz
  ka raita, 40
Bhune tamatar ka ras, 13
Bhune tamatar ka
  shorva, 22
Bhuni sabzi milwan, 8-9
Bhutte ka salat, 29
Black pepper, xviii
Black salt, xviii
Blender, xxv
Butter, spicy garlic, 164

c

Calcutta egg rolls, 57
Cardamom, xviii
Carom seeds, xix
Cauliflower florets
  marinated in yogurt
  and spices, 133-134
Cayenne pepper, xix
Chane ki tikki, 139-140
Chatniwale seekh kabobs,
  90
Chicken, 53-81
  Chicken breast and
    pineapple chunks
    marinated in almonds,
    cashew nuts, coconut,
    and cream, 63
  Chicken breast marinated
    in a paste of sweet red
    peppers, onion, and
    spices, 11

Chicken breast marinated
  in cardamom, black
  pepper, yogurt, and
  fresh coriander, 65-66
Chicken breast marinated
  in fresh coriander, ginger, and lemon juice, 10
Chicken breast marinated
  in soy sauce, vinegar,
  sesame oil, and spices,
  66-67
Chicken breast marinated
  in thickened yogurt and
  spices, 62
Chicken breast marinated
  with tomatoes and
  spices, and grilled with
  fresh peaches, 70
Chicken breast marinated
  with yogurt, cardamom,
  and fennel, 64-65
Chicken drumsticks
  marinated in yogurt,
  spices, and herbs, 72-73
Chicken marinated with
  sautéed onions, 74-75
Chicken marinated with
  sautéed onions, vinegar,
  and spices, 76-77
Chicken marinated in
  green chilies and
  tamarind, 78-79
Chicken marinated in
  puréed green tomatoes
  and sour cream, 73

Chicken (*continued*)
Chicken marinated in
sautéed onions, toma-
toes, and spices, 68–69
Chicken marinated in
tamarind, ground fennel
seeds, and ginger, 75–76
Chicken marinated with
spinach, fresh coriander,
and spices, 71
Chicken thighs marinated
in sour cream and
spices, and stuffed
with sautéed onion,
mushrooms, and bread
crumbs, 80–81
Grilled chicken salad
with tomatoes and
green onions in a spicy
yogurt dressing, 28
Ground-chicken kabobs
minced with cashew
nuts and spices, 59–60
Ground-chicken kabobs
marinated with sun-
dried tomatoes, roasted
peppers, and sautéed
onions, 60–61
Rice cooked with grilled
chicken and garam
masala, 159–160
Rice cooked with grilled
chicken curry, 160–161
Skewers of ground
chicken marinated with
fried onion and dried
fenugreek leaves, 58–59
Wraps stuffed with eggs
and chicken, 57
Chickpea flour, xxii
Chickpeas, croquettes of
mashed, with potatoes
and spices, 139–140
Chilies, green, xix
Chili chicken, 78–79
Chinese parsley. *See*
Coriander, fresh
Cholam soup, 23
Chutneys. *See* Raitas and
Chutneys
Cilantro. *See* Coriander,
fresh

Cinnamon, xix
Cloves, xx
Coconut milk, xxii
Coffee grinder, electric,
xxv
Cooking techniques
Cottage cheese, xxvi
Dry-roasting spices,
xxvi–xxvii
Garam masala, xxvii
Coriander, fresh, xxiii
Coriander seeds, ground,
xx
Corn
Grilled corn and onion
soup in a coconut and
cream broth, 23
Grilled corn and roasted
red peppers tossed
with onions in a lemon
and roasted-spice
dressing, 29
Roasted buttered corn
with salt and lemon
juice, 7
Skewers of mashed
potatoes and corn,
138–139
Cottage cheese
Cooking techniques
for, xxvi
Cottage cheese marinated
in fresh coriander, mint,
and spices, 125–126
Cottage cheese marinated
in spices, fresh corian-
der, and olive oil,
132–133
Cottage cheese marinated
in yogurt and spices,
123–124
Croquettes of mashed
potatoes, cottage
cheese, and roasted
peanuts, 137–138
Grilled cottage cheese
and green peppers
marinated and served
in a sauce of cashew
nuts, dried fenugreek
leaves, tomatoes, and
sour cream, 128–129

Grilled cottage cheese
served in a tomato
cream sauce with
sautéed onion and
green pepper, 130–131
Crispy potatoes marinated
in spices, fresh
coriander, and olive
oil, 132–133
Crispy shrimp marinated
with chickpea flour,
eggs, and sour cream,
12–13
Croquettes
Croquettes of mashed
chickpeas, potatoes, and
spices, 139–140
Croquettes of mashed
potatoes, cottage
cheese, and roasted
peanuts, 137–138
Croquettes of mashed
potatoes stuffed with
green peas, ginger, and
spices, 141–142
Cucumber with grilled
potatoes, onion, and
tomatoes in yogurt, 43
Cuisines, Indian and
Middle Eastern, xii
Cumin seeds, whole and
ground, xx
Curry, about, 68
Curry leaves, xxiv
ɖ
Dalchini, xix
Dhaniya murgh tikka, 10
Dhaniye aur dahi ka
masala, 170–171
Dips, 50–51. *See also* Raitas
and Chutneys
Drinks. *See* Appetizers
and Drinks
Dry-roasting spices,
xxvi–xxvii
ε̄
Eggplant
Baby eggplant cooked
in a sweet-and-sour
tamarind-fennel sauce
with grilled apples,
136–137

Eggplant slices grilled
with spiced oil, 124
Roasted eggplant, onions,
and tomatoes sautéed
with spices, 134–135
Roasted eggplant with
sautéed onion in
yogurt, 39
Eggs
Wraps stuffed with egg
and chicken, 57
Elaichi, xviii
f
Farghana, xii
Fennel seeds, xx
Fenugreek leaves, dried,
xxiv
Fenugreek seeds, xxi
Fish. *See also* Seafood
Fish fillet marinated and
served in a sauce of
ground mustard seeds,
spices, yogurt, onion,
and tomatoes, 107–108
Fish fillet marinated in
lemon juice and spices,
served in a sauce of
sautéed onion, coconut,
tomato, and spices,
112–113
Fish fillet marinated
in sour cream and
spices, 105
Fish steaks coated with a
sauce of coconut, fresh
coriander, and spices,
114–115
Fish steaks marinated in
fresh coriander, dried
fenugreek leaves, and
spices, 106
Fish steaks marinated in
tamarind and toasted
ground spices, 110–111
Food processor, xxv
ḡ
Garam masala, xxi, xxvii
Garlic, roasted, in spicy
yogurt, 15
Gosht awadh, 98–99
Gosht biryani, 162–163
Gosht lajawab, 96–97

Gosht roghan josh, 94-95
Green chilies, xix
Green mangoes. *See*
    Mangoes
Green peppers
  Green peppers stuffed
      with spicy sautéed
      potatoes, 143-144
  Grilled cottage cheese
      and green peppers
      marinated and served in
      a sauce of cashew nuts,
      dried fenugreek leaves,
      tomatoes, and cream,
      128-129
Green tomato chutney,
    sweet and sour, with
    dates, 44
Grilled breaded salmon
    steaks marinated in
    olive oil, lemon juice,
    herbs, and spices,
    104-105
Grilled corn and onion
    soup in a coconut and
    cream broth, 23
Grilled corn and roasted
    red peppers tossed
    with onions in a lemon
    and roasted-spice
    dressing, 29
Grilled cottage cheese and
    green peppers mari-
    nated and served in a
    sauce of cashew nuts,
    dried fenugreek leaves,
    tomatoes, and cream,
    128-129
Grilled cubes of cottage
    cheese served in a
    tomato cream sauce
    with sautéed onion
    and green pepper,
    130-131
Grilled ground meat
    kabobs tossed in a
    thickened yogurt,
    mint, and coriander
    dressing, 34
Grilled mixed vegetable
    soup in chicken
    broth, 25

Grilled mixed vegetables
    cooked with rice,
    coconut milk, and
    spices, 154-156
Grilled mushrooms
    marinated with spices,
    lemon juice, and fresh
    coriander, 6
Grilled mushrooms
    served in a roasted
    tomato-tamarind broth
    with black pepper,
    20-21
Grilled mushrooms served
    in a sauce of sautéed
    onion, tomatoes, and
    cream, 149-150
Grilled pappadums, 9
Grilled pumpkin in spiced
    yogurt, 41
Grilled pumpkin soup with
    cream and scallions,
    26-27
Grilled scallops and green
    mangoes tossed with
    shredded cabbage and
    red onion in a mustard
    lemon dressing, 30-32
Grilled zucchini in lightly
    spiced yogurt, 38
Ground-chicken kabobs
    marinated with sun-
    dried tomatoes, roasted
    peppers, and sautéed
    onions, 60-61
Ground-chicken kabobs
    minced with cashew
    nuts and spices, 59-60
Ground meat kabobs
    wrapped in tortillas and
    grilled, 95-96
Guchchi ki sabzi, 149-150
Guchchi masaledaar, 6
Guchchi wala pulao,
    158-159

h
Hara aam, xxii-xxiii
Hara dhaniya, xxiii
Hara murga, 73
Hare aam aur bundgobhi
    ka salat, 30-32
Hare aam ki chatni, 48

Hare tamatar ki chatni, 44
Hari machali, 106
Hari mirch, xix
Herbs, xxiii-xxiv

ī
Imli, xxiii
Imliwali machali, 110-111
Indian hospitality, 4-5
Indus River Valley, xii

j̄
Jeera, sabut aur pisa, xx
Jhatpat tamatar wali chatni,
    46-47
Jhinga moongphaliwala,
    115-116
Jhinga patia, 116-117
Jhinge au simla mirch ka
    salat, 33
Juice of roasted tomatoes
    with cumin and
    Tabasco, 13

k
Kabob tamatari, 60-61
Kaddoo ka raita, 41
Kaddoo ka shorva, 26-27
Kaddoo ki sabzi, 145-146
Kaju methi paneer ke tikke,
    128-129
Kaju reshmi seekh kabobs,
    59-60
Kala namak, xviii
Kalan mullagatanni, 20-21
Kali mirch, xviii
Kalonji, xxi
Karara jhinga, 12-13
Karipatta, xxiv
Kashmiri murgh chaval,
    159-160
Kashmiri murgh elaichi,
    64-65
Kasoori methi, xxiv
Kathi kabobs, 95-96
Khatti meethi tamatar
    ki chatni, 45-46

l
Lamb, 83-99
  Grilled ground meat
      kabobs tossed in a
      thickened yogurt,
      mint, and coriander
      dressing, 34

Ground meat kabobs
    wrapped in tortillas and
    grilled, 95-96
Lamb marinated in
    coconut, tamarind, and
    spices, 92-93
Lamb marinated in
    pickling spices, onions,
    and vinegar, 91-92
Lamb marinated in
    yogurt, almonds, and
    ground fennel seeds,
    94-95
Lamb marinated with
    onion, fenugreek, and
    spices, 96-97
Lamb marinated with
    sautéed onions, yogurt,
    spices, and fennel seeds,
    98-99
Rice cooked with spicy
    grilled lamb curry,
    162-163
Skewered lamb kabobs
    ground with spinach
    and spices, 88-89
Skewers of ground lamb
    flavored with dried
    fenugreek leaves and
    spices, 86-87
Skewers of ground lamb
    marinated with fresh
    herbs, 90
Skewers of ground lamb
    marinated with fried
    onions and almonds,
    87-88

m̄
Machali masala, 104-105
Majhige, 15
Makhani tamatar ka
    masala, 167
Mangoes
  Green cooking mango,
      xxii-xxiii
  Grilled scallops and
      green mangoes
      tossed with shredded
      cabbage and red
      onion in a mustard
      lemon dressing,
      30-32

Mangoes (*continued*)
   Roasted green mango chutney with fresh herbs, chilies, and roasted garlic, 48
   Roasted green mango juice, 14
   Roasted green mangoes in a spicy sweet-and-sour sauce, 49
Methi, xxi
Methiwala gosht, 86–87
Mili juli sabzi ka shorva, 25
Mint, fresh and dried, xxiv
Mint yogurt dip with roasted garlic, 50
Mixed vegetables
   Grilled mixed vegetable soup in chicken broth, 25
   Grilled mixed vegetables cooked with rice, coconut milk, and spices, 154–156
   Mixed vegetables marinated in spicy oil and lemon juice, 8–9
Moghlai, xiii
Moghlai tikka, 63
Moghuls, xii–xiii
"Mulligatawny" soup, 20
Murgh biryani, 160–161
Murgh kashmiri, 75–76
Murgh ka soola, 74–75
Murgh kasoori, 58–59
Murgh tikka, 62
Mushrooms
   Grilled mushrooms marinated with spices, lemon juice, and fresh coriander, 6
   Grilled mushrooms served in a roasted tomato-tamarind broth with black pepper, 20–21
   Grilled mushrooms served in a sauce of sautéed onion, tomatoes, and cream, 149–150

Portobello mushrooms marinated in vinegar and spices, stuffed with spiced feta cheese, 147–148
Mustard seeds, xxi
Mutton, about, 84–85

n

Nariyal ka doodh, xxii

o

Onion seeds, xxi

p

Paneer, xxvi, 123
Paneer durbari, 130–131
Panna, 14
Pappadums, grilled, 9
Patla, xiv
Patra ni machali, 114–115
Podhini, taza aur sookha, xxiv
Portobello mushrooms marinated in vinegar and spices, stuffed with spiced feta cheese, 147–148
Potatoes
   Crispy potatoes marinated in spices, fresh coriander, and olive oil, 132–133
   Croquettes of mashed chickpeas, potatoes, and spices, 139–140
   Croquettes of mashed potatoes, cottage cheese, and roasted peanuts, 137–138
   Croquettes of mashed potatoes stuffed with green peas, ginger, and spices, 141–142
   Green peppers stuffed with spicy, sautéed potatoes, 143–144
   Roasted potatoes in spiced yogurt, 42
   Skewers of mashed potatoes and corn, 138–139
Preparation necessary for Indian grill cooking, xvii–xxvii

Pumpkin
   Grilled pumpkin in spiced yogurt, 41
   Grilled pumpkin soup with cream and scallions, 26–27
   Roasted pumpkin with onions and fenugreek seeds, 145–146

q

Quick grilled tomato salsa, 46–47

r

Rai, xxi
Raitas and Chutneys, 35–51
   Cucumber with grilled potatoes, onion, and tomatoes in yogurt, 43
   Grilled pumpkin in spiced yogurt, 41
   Grilled zucchini in lightly spiced yogurt, 38
   Mint yogurt dip with roasted garlic, 50
   Quick grilled tomato salsa, 46–47
   Roasted eggplant with sautéed onion in yogurt, 39
   Roasted green mango chutney with fresh herbs, chilies, and roasted garlic, 48
   Roasted green mangoes in a spicy sweet-and-sour sauce, 49
   Roasted potatoes in spiced yogurt, 42
   Roasted red pepper and garlic yogurt dip, 51
   Roasted tomatoes and onion in yogurt spiced with mint and roasted cumin seeds, 40
   Sweet-and-sour green tomato chutney with dates, 44
   Sweet, sour, and spicy tomato chutney with ginger, 45

Rasam, 24
Red peppers
   Grilled corn and roasted red peppers, tossed with onions in a lemon and roasted-spice dressing, 29
   Roasted red pepper and garlic yogurt dip, 51
   Shrimp and roasted red pepper salad with a sour cream, honey, and lime dressing, 33
Rice, 151–164
   Basmati rice, xxii
   Grilled mixed vegetables cooked with rice, coconut milk, and spices, 154–156
   Rice cooked with grilled chicken and garam masala, 159–160
   Rice cooked with grilled chicken curry, 160–161
   Rice cooked with grilled mushrooms and sweet red peppers, 158–159
   Rice cooked with peas in a roasted tomato purée, 156–157
   Rice cooked with spicy grilled lamb curry, 162–163
Roasted buttered corn with salt and lemon juice, 7
Roasted eggplant, onions, and tomatoes sautéed with spices, 134–135
Roasted eggplant with sautéed onion in yogurt, 39
Roasted garlic in spicy yogurt, 15
Roasted green mango chutney with fresh herbs, chilies, and roasted garlic, 48
Roasted green mango juice, 14
Roasted green mangoes in a spicy sweet-and-sour sauce, 49

Roasted potatoes in spiced yogurt, 42
Roasted pumpkin with onions and fenugreek seeds, 145-146
Roasted red pepper and garlic yogurt dip, 51
Roasted-tomato soup with cumin and fresh coriander, 22
Roasted tomatoes and onion in yogurt spiced with mint and roasted cumin seeds, 40

S

Saag seekh kabobs, 88-89
Salads, 17-19, 28-34
    Grilled chicken salad with tomatoes and green onions in a spicy yogurt dressing, 28
    Grilled corn and roasted red peppers tossed with onions in a lemon and roasted-spice dressing, 29
    Grilled ground meat kabobs tossed in a thickened yogurt, meat, and coriander dressing, 34
    Grilled scallops and green mangoes tossed with shredded cabbage and red onion in a mustard lemon dressing, 30-32
    Shrimp and roasted red pepper salad with a sour cream, honey, and lime dressing, 33
    Sweet potato chunks tossed with spices and lemon juice, 32
Salat-e-kabob, 34
Salmon
    Grilled breaded salmon steaks marinated in olive oil, lemon juice, herbs, and spices, 104-105

Salmon steaks marinated in lemon juice and spices, served in a sauce of sautéed onion, fresh coriander, and tomatoes, 108-110
Salsa, quick grilled tomato, 46-47
Sauces, 165-171
    Tomato sauce with butter and cream, 167
    Tomato sauce with cashew nuts and sour cream, 169
    Tomato sauce with fenugreek and cream, 168
    Yogurt sauce with fresh coriander and ginger, 170-171
Saunf, xx
    Scallops and mangoes, grilled, tossed with shredded cabbage and red onion in a mustard lemon dressing, 30-32
Seafood, 101-118
    Crispy shrimp marinated with chickpea flour, eggs, and sour cream, 12-13
    Fish fillet marinated and served in a sauce of ground mustard seeds, spices, yogurt, onion, and tomatoes, 107-108
    Fish fillet marinated in lemon juice and spices, served in a sauce of sautéed onion, coconut, tomato, and spices, 112-113
    Fish fillet marinated in sour cream and spices, 105
    Fish steaks coated with a sauce of coconut, fresh coriander, and spices, 114-115
    Fish steaks marinated in fresh coriander, dried fenugreek leaves, and spices, 106

Fish steaks marinated in tamarind and toasted ground spices, 110-111
    Grilled breaded salmon steaks marinated in olive oil, lemon juice, herbs, and spices, 104-105
    Grilled scallops and green mangoes tossed with shredded cabbage and red onion in a mustard lemon dressing, 30-32
    Salmon steaks marinated in lemon juice and spices, served in a sauce of sautéed onion, fresh coriander, and tomatoes, 108-110
    Shrimp and roasted red pepper salad with a sour cream, honey, and lime dressing, 33
    Shrimp marinated in thickened yogurt and spices, lightly breaded and grilled with onion, 118
    Shrimp marinated with ground roasted peanuts, yogurt, and spices, and skewered with tomatoes, 115-116
    Sweet, hot, and sour shrimp marinated and served in a sauce of onion, tomato, spices, and tamarind, 116-117
Shakarkandi ki chaat, 32
Sherbat, 5
Shrimp
    Crispy shrimp marinated with chickpea flour, eggs, and sour cream, 12-13
    Shrimp and roasted red pepper salad with a sour cream, honey, and lime dressing, 33

Shrimp marinated in thickened yogurt and spices, lightly breaded and grilled with onion, 118
Shrimp marinated with ground roasted peanuts, yogurt, and spices, and skewered with tomatoes, 115-116
Sweet, hot, and sour shrimp marinated and served in a sauce of onions, tomato, spices, and tamarind, 116-117
Sindhi elaichi murgh, 65-66
Sindhi hariyali machali, 108-110
Skewers, xxv
Skewered lamb kabobs ground with spinach and spices, 88-89
Skewers of ground chicken marinated with fried onion and dried fenugreek leaves, 58-59
Skewers of ground lamb flavored with dried fenugreek leaves and spices, 86-87
Skewers of ground lamb marinated with fresh herbs, 90
Skewers of ground lamb marinated with fried onions and almonds, 87-88
Skewers of mashed corn and potatoes, 138-139
Sookha dhaniya, xx
Sorse maach, 107-108
Soups, 17-27
    Grilled corn and onion soup in a coconut and cream broth, 23
    Grilled mixed vegetable soup in chicken broth, 25

Soups (*continued*)
  Grilled mushrooms
    served in a roasted
    tomato-tamarind broth
    with black pepper,
    20–21
  Grilled pumpkin
    soup with cream and
    scallions, 26–27
  Roasted-tomato soup
    with cumin and fresh
    coriander, 22
  Spicy grilled tomato
    soup, 24–25
Soya murgh, 66–67
Spices, dry roasting,
  xxvi–xxvii
Spices, essential, xvii–xxi
Spicy garlic butter, 164
Spicy grilled tomato
  soup, 24–25
Subz biryani, 154–156
Sweet-and-sour green
  tomato chutney with
  dates, 44
Sweet, hot, and sour shrimp
  marinated and served in
  a sauce of onions,
  tomato, spices, and
  tamarind, 116–117
Sweet potatoes tossed
  with spices and lemon
  juice, 32
Sweet, sour, and spicy
  tomato chutney with
  ginger, 45–46

t

Tamarind, xxiii
Tamatar ka pulao, 156–157
Tamatar kaju ka masala, 169
Tamatar methi ka
  masala, 168
Tandoori cooking,
  discussion of, xi–xvi
Tandoori gobhi, 133–134
Tandoori jhinga, 118
Tandoori machali, 105
Tandoori murgh, 72–73
Tandoori murgh kari,
  68–69

Tandoori murgh salat, 28
Tandoori murgh vindaloo,
  76–77
Tandoori paneer, 123–124
Tandoori paneer
  chatniwali, 125–126
Thayir pachadi, 43
Thenga erachi, 92–93
Thenga meen, 112–113
Tikkas, 10, 62
Tomato chutney
  Sweet-and-sour green
    tomato chutney with
    dates, 44
  Sweet, sour, and spicy
    tomato chutney with
    ginger, 45–46
Tomato sauce with butter
  and cream, 167
Tomato sauce with
  cashew nuts and sour
  cream, 169
Tomato sauce with
  fenugreek and cream,
  168
Tomatoes
  Juice of roasted tomatoes
    with cumin and
    Tabasco, 13
  Quick grilled tomato
    salsa, 46–47
  Roasted-tomato soup
    with cumin and fresh
    coriander, 22
  Spicy grilled tomato
    soup, 24–25
  Sweet and sour green
    tomato chutney with
    dates, 44
  Sweet, sour, and spicy
    tomato chutney with
    ginger, 45–46

v

Vegetables, 119–150. *See
  also* vegetables by name
Baby eggplant coated in a
  sweet-and-sour
  tamarind-fennel sauce
  served with grilled
  apples, 136–137

Cauliflower florets
  marinated in yogurt
  and spices, 133–134
Cottage cheese marinated
  in fresh coriander, mint,
  and spices, 125–126
Cottage cheese marinated
  in green chilies, ginger,
  garlic, fresh coriander,
  and soy sauce, 126–127
Cottage cheese marinated
  in yogurt and spices,
  123–124
Crispy potatoes mari-
  nated in spices, fresh
  coriander, and olive oil,
  132–133
Croquettes of mashed
  chickpeas, potatoes, and
  spices, 139–140
Croquettes of mashed
  potatoes, cottage
  cheese, and roasted
  peanuts, 137–138
Croquettes of mashed
  potatoes stuffed with
  green peas, ginger, and
  spices, 141–142
Eggplant slices grilled
  with spiced oil, 124
Green peppers stuffed
  with spicy sautéed
  potatoes, 143–144
Grilled cottage cheese
  and green peppers mar-
  inated and served in a
  sauce of cashew nuts,
  dried fenugreek leaves,
  tomatoes, and cream,
  128–129
Grilled cottage cheese
  served in a tomato
  cream sauce with
  sautéed onion and
  green pepper,
  130–131
Grilled mushrooms
  served in a sauce of
  sautéed onion, toma-
  toes, and cream, 149

Mixed vegetables
  marinated in spicy
  oil and lemon juice,
  8–9
Portobello mushrooms
  marinated in vinegar
  and spices, stuffed with
  spiced feta cheese,
  147–148
Roasted eggplant,
  onions, and tomatoes
  sautéed with spices,
  134–135
Roasted pumpkin
  cooked with onions
  and fenugreek seeds,
  145–146
Skewers of mashed
  corn and potatoes,
  138–139

w

Wraps stuffed with egg
  and chicken, 57

y

Yogurt
  Mint yogurt dip with
    roasted garlic, 50
  Roasted garlic in spicy
    yogurt, 15
  Roasted potatoes in
    spiced yogurt, 42
  Roasted red pepper
    and garlic yogurt dip,
    51
  Yogurt relishes. *See*
    Raitas and Chutneys
  Yogurt sauce with
    fresh coriander and
    ginger, 170–171

z

Zucchini
  Grilled zucchini in
    lightly spiced yogurt,
    38
  Zucchini ka raita, 38

about the author

Smita **C**handra was born and raised in India, where she learned several generations' worth of culinary traditions. She has lived in North America since 1985. She is the author of a previous cookbook, *From Bengal to Punjab*, and currently lives with her husband and two sons in Toronto, where she teaches Indian cooking and works as a freelance writer.